THE WISE VIRGIN

for Tia

ANNIE WILSON

The Wise Virgin

The Missing Link
Between Men and Women

Foreword by
LYALL WATSON

Published by
TURNSTONE BOOKS
37 Upper Addison Gardens
London W14 8AJ

© 1979 Annie Wilson

Hardcover ISBN 0 85500 096 1
Paperback ISBN 0 85500 103 8

First published 1979

Typeset in 11/12½ Baskerville by
Saildean Limited, Kingston, Surrey
Printed by Lowe & Brydone Limited
Thetford, Norfolk
Bound by Biddles Bookbinders
Kings Lynn, Norfolk
Paper Supplied by
Frank Grunfeld Limited, London

Contents

FOREWORD by Lyall Watson   7

One   PERSONAL CALL
         Signposts towards you   11
         Where there's a will   37
         A path with heart   51

Two: NOTES TOWARDS A SUPREME
         FICTION
         It must be abstract   63
         It must change   75
         It must give pleasure   89

Three: INNOCENCE AND EXPERIENCE
         Education   103
         Astrology   115
         Psychology   124
         Art   132
         Healing   140

Four: THE HEART OF THE MATTER
         Down to earth   153
         Up to earth   166
         The Holy Grail   177

BOOKS THAT HELPED TO CLEAR THE PATH   190

Acknowledgements

my special love and thanks to:

Isobel McGilvray
   and to
Diana Becchetti
Lorraine Gill
Liz Greene
Lynice Yates

my thanks, too, for the wisdom of:

Barbara Somers and Ian Gordon-Brown
   in Transpersonal Psychology
Margaret Rose in Mythology in Literature

and for the support of:

Olga Kerek
Richard Gannon
Andrew Lyall-Watson
Mary Pyke

FOREWORD

by

Lyall Watson

In a desert corner of Arizona, close to the Mexican border, live a tuneful people. The Papago Indians today wear white man's clothing, build adobe houses and drive across dry Sonora in dusty pick-up trucks; but beneath these modern trappings little has changed. These are a gentle, poetic people who never raise their voices – even the lustiest men speak the soft, sliding, whispered syllables of the old Aztec tongue in a smiling undertone. All their movements are deliberate, tempered by the desert heat to a slow swinging cadence that makes us look swift and jerky and nervous. And they are always laughing in a tender loving ripple that flows through every conversation like background music.

The Papago fought when they had to, striking back at the wolfish Apache on their northern boundary when occasion demanded, but there was never any glory in war. A warrior who killed, retired immediately from the conflict and was not considered a man to be fêted, but one to be avoided at all costs until he had become purified by an elaborate ritual lasting sixteen days. Battle was an ugly duty to be performed solely for the sake of the tribe, and the only reward was the possibility of a dream. To a worthy man, who showed all proper humility, there might come a dream – and a dream always contained a song.

Song is the most precious possession of the Papago and the power of song is an honour to be earned. Singing is a method of magic which calls on the resources of nature through which magic can be worked, but only if the words of the song are true and beautiful and if the singing is done, as it should be, at the right time and with the proper ritual, on behalf of all the people. Even now the most honoured members of the tribe are still those who can compose and sing the best songs. A practical man, a successful farmer or businessman, is valued only if he is also a poet – someone who can be wistful, solemn, humourous and shy; who can conjure up the warmth of a mother's love, or weep in sympathy with a lonely child.

In the company of these people I am not only jerky, but woefully incomplete. Papago men – squat, broad-faced and dark – have a looming masculine presence that makes me feel effete; but at the same time they exude compassion and sensitivity in a way that is distinctly feminine. I envy them their easy equilibrium, because I believe, as Annie Wilson does, that the key to true individuation lies in balance, and that a man cannot be properly masculine until he discovers and assimilates the feminine side of his own nature. But for myself, and I suspect for many others caught in the same cultural dilemma, this is by no means easy.

It is hard to avoid role-playing. It is difficult to trust intuition and to leave things to chance. It is almost impossible to rely on the relatedness of all things and to let our intellects be guided and informed by pure imagination. But this is what the Papago do, and this is exactly what we all need to learn to do if we are to have a chance of becoming truly attuned.

So I celebrate Annie's adoption of the role of The Wise Virgin; I endorse her assertion that 'the feminine principle is the matrix of life from which the seed springs'; and I find myself inspired by her to take responsibility for balancing my own books and being. May her lamp always be filled with the essential oils of awareness.

Welcome, whether you be male or female, to the more than ever vital game of Find the Lady.

Lyall Watson

1

Personal Call

*'There was a young man who said ' Though
it seems that I know that I know
What I would like to see
Is the 'I' that knows me
When I know that I know that I know.''*

Alan Watts in *'The Taboo Against Knowing Who You Are'*

Signposts towards you

*"A kind of electric current flows into us
and we feel capable of accomplishing
what we want to do".*

Laurens Van der Post in *Vogue,* January 1977

A Seeker After Truth? I would never have put it quite like
that. But at every step of my life I have wished there to be
something more. At the age of eighteen I knew that if I did
not do something about myself, I would die. I hated what I
was. I thought I knew nothing, felt I was nothing, and was
certain I could relate to no one, least of all to myself.

The struggle for survival was on – simply to become
someone I liked. It hurt like hell; there was so much work to
do and I had to do it for myself. I began, at that moment of
decision, by writing down the first five things I was determined to achieve. Quite silly things, but I made myself
achieve them. And it went on from there. At twenty-seven I
realised, on reflection, that I had somehow, strangely, managed to achieve those things I had set myself to do. In my own
way I had socially and financially achieved the things I had
dreamed of. I sat back and looked at where I was. It occurred
to me that the work, which I loved, had never actually been
important for itself, only for the personal growth it had given
me. After all those years of struggle to reach that place, the
place meant nothing. The value was in travelling there. I was
there because I had been forced to survive. There had been

no alternative. The route was inevitable; a path to a goal.

But does the path stop? I knew I could now cope with almost any situation in which I set myself. I had my own power and position. I knew my personal boundaries intimately and suspected my professional place, but ambition in the old sense seemed pointless. There had to be something more. I tried to talk about this sensing of 'more', but it had no words – it just was. 'Progress' was the only way I could describe it. A path that goes on. But I had no idea how or where it went.

As the months went on, the certainty grew inside me. There *must* be something more. I was bursting at the seams of my own world, but nothing would give. The trapdoor above me was locked. There was no way out because what could there be that was more? I had it all. All that I knew.

One day 'by chance', a publicity sheet arrived on my desk. The article, about an astrologer with a reputation for success, persuaded me to have my tarot cards read. It was the most effective psychological boost I have ever experienced. I came out bubbling. It was as though something, somewhere, knew I existed. I don't think anything very specific happened, not really, but it left me with an overwhelming sense of possibility. The tone of his reading seemed in harmony with my life; or at least with its potential. It felt right. It suggested I did have a future.

Something was triggered. All I can say is that I began to feel a kind of 'certainty', a 'knowing' about 'something'.

Almost two years later I went to a second astrologer who drew my horoscope. I remember only that she told me my life over the next three years would be difficult because it would be influenced by Saturn. "If you get through the next three years," she told me, "at least you will have learned something!" Nothing exceptionally helpful, but from that moment I felt she had confirmed what I already knew. Now I knew that I knew something.

In those early days I found that only two friends, both of them women, could grasp what I meant. Not by anything I could say; the contents of the words would not have made sense to anyone else. It was more a communication through feeling; a shared experience of a sense of energy. I could sense, just by being with someone, whether or not they were aware of this 'extra dimension'. We could 'talk' about it for hours and when we were done, much in life that had seemed important before began to seem irrelevant.

Intellectually I knew nothing about alternative philosophies or psychologies. At that time I felt that reading such things had little point unless they confirmed what I already knew. Knowing things intellectually seemed immaterial. I felt it was more important to trust this sense of 'knowing'. At that time too there was a general increase in interest in occult phenomena. Although there is a link here in the sense that the occult deals with things that are 'hidden', this approach also seemed irrelevant. The 'knowing' was far more encompassing, more reassuring and much more universal.

Since none of us had a religion, we hesitated to link it to anything religious, but somehow the term was relevant. A kind of religious 'goodness and purpose' about something we could not see or understand or even begin to plan on using. It was something bursting to be fulfilled; a role one had to play. But how or when, we didn't know. Nor was it only on a personal level; it had a much wider, more universal significance. We felt it had to do with evolution and change. With the importance of now. With the crumbling of satisfaction with the material world. But its main ingredient was an overwhelming optimism, an enormous sense of joy at this new thing and its positive direction. The sum of the energy generated by all our 'certainty', was certainly greater than its parts.

For me personally I knew it was to mean a huge amount of change. If any of 'this thing' was true, it must certainly mean *that,* because the last thing it offered was security. It was a lesson in trust and intuition, and above all, in having the courage to jump. I was scared, but the path had been set. The 'carrots' of coincidence began to dangle and I began to know in a strange way what was going to happen to me.

That period of 'knowing' was a kind of Peak Experience. It has taken me three chaotic years to discover just a little of what that means.

In the beginning, I thought I was alone with my overwhelming certainty, my sense of something more. No one else in my world could feel it. And no matter how hard I tried to explain, the words said nothing. But the trigger had been sprung and the search had begun. It was wonderful because it was 'right', and miserable because it was lonely. I couldn't turn back because 'fate' wouldn't let me. Finally, of course, I discovered it wasn't only me. Other people had reached similar starting points; each in their own strange way.

From these I choose five women to weave through the fabric of my book. I choose women, but for another weaver at any other loom, the choice might have fallen on men. And, in order to see what I believe to be the meaning of the completed pattern, I think it important to look at each of the five component threads in isolation.

LIZ GREENE is thirty-one, a successful astrologer, psychologist and writer.* She is slim and dark and very much at home on a lecture platform from which she transmits a cool and attractive intelligence. From an American Jewish, lower-middle-class background with a conventional suburban structured morality, she has no memory before the age of five; "which testifies to the atmosphere – it was pretty hideous, absolutely neurotic." Liz's mother was a brilliant, highly-educated woman who consciously did her best to be a wife and mother, but unconsciously resented some of the roles thrust upon her. An unhappy woman, in furious conflict, she saw an opportunity to live through her children what she couldn't accomplish herself. Her father was introverted and withdrawn, a totally repressed man who had financial

---

* *Saturn: a new look at an old devil.* Samuel Weiser Inc. (1976)
Relating: a guide to living with others on a small planet
Coventure, London (1977)
Looking at the Mind, Coventure, London (1977)
Looking at Astrology, Coventure, London (1977)

difficulties at the beginning of the marriage and was ashamed of not being able to support his family adequately. His only outlet was in violence, primarily towards Liz, for reasons she understands. He had to hit someone, she says, or he would have exploded. It forced her into her own world.

Her mother took Liz, who was musically gifted at four, to piano teachers who thought her a prodigy. At the age of five she was also good at art and was pronounced a genius who should become an artist. No one thought to ask her whether or not she wanted to be one. She was a gifted child with a high IQ who could read and write at the age of three. "But *who* I was, never registered. Only what I could accomplish and to what use it could be put. If I did well I received reward, money and gifts. If I did badly, I got criticism."

But, as she says, her parents did not drink and were never divorced, so to all intents and purposes it was a reasonable family life. "But I remember far back vowing that whatever I did it was not going to be like this. I was not going to live my life like these people."

Above everything she had to be alone, to get away from people. Her first survival technique was to develop ways of going uphill against her mother's pressure. At five a school psychologist had said she was such an introverted child, her mother should push her into society. "She began to invite all the neighbourhood children around to little parties and I hated it. The more I was pushed the more I turned to fantasies, fairytales and legends. I acted out myths and stories like King Arthur and the Holy Grail. I was Guinevere, my brother was Parsifal. I had some companionship with him because he was being treated in a similar way. Most of the time I climbed trees and would sit there for hours. Nature kept me sane, animals and plants, things that came up out of the earth. Plus drawing and reading."

The pressure built up, until around the age of fourteen she began to rebel. In an act of classic teenage rebellion, she put her foot down firmly and refused to do the things demanded. "Everyone was astonished. People thought I was such a quiet person. I hated them for what they did to me, because they wouldn't leave me alone to be myself. I could see my mother's drive and tried to tell her in the language I knew. But she couldn't accept it."

By nineteen, at university, she was exploding. "I was becoming completely unglued," says Liz. "I finally broke down, locked in a one-room basement flat, until after a month alone I began to crawl out,"

She was studying academic psychology; an eighth of her time spent at classes making notes, the rest in torment. Her break-down began in time for exams which, but for a sympathetic tutor, she should have failed. Everything was black.

"And then someone took me to an astrologer. The woman only did a very brief chart reading, but suddenly it made me realise that something was going on here and I was determined to find out what. I went home knowing that she couldn't have figured out all that on her own. You can pick up a lot from clues such as the way people sit, but she had given me too much information. She went on about Scorpio and how difficult it was to have as an ascendant sign because of the intensity and constant bottling-up of emotions and the darkness associated with it. It struck me that what had previously been my own burden was a temperament other people shared. Just to hear someone say that it was all right, was a relief, after my parents' criticism that my behaviour was too emotional. She talked of my parents and said neither had ever known me, and that Saturn in Leo meant I had too much pride, and that I needed to learn to love people more. She knew about my artistic abilities."

At this point Liz did not wonder what astrology was and she had no interest in the philosophy or theory. She just knew she wanted to read charts. "I tried to ask her to give me lessons and at first she said she would like to teach me because she thought that one day I would be gifted. I couldn't pay for lessons from her and she said I could come instead to clean her office."

The first thing Liz did was to look for her chart. "There were certain things she hadn't told me and I felt she had taken a dislike to me. She said she had lost my chart but I knew she had hidden it. I thought she knew something I had a right to know. Looking back I sense it was jealousy.

"I cleaned her office for two Saturdays in a row, but the lessons never materialised. On the second occasion she gave me money for floor wax and I bought a smaller bottle than she had asked for. She threw a fit about me being a thief. I couldn't understand this. Obviously I was going to give her the change, but she said she never wanted to see me again. Something about me freaked her out, but she is a well-known astrologer now and I doubt she would remember the incident.

"So I borrowed a bunch of books and taught myself. The implications didn't hit me. I just thought, my god this works. I didn't have difficulty in accepting it as some people do, I saw no reason why it shouldn't work. It told you about human behaviour, it gave an insight into people."

Originally she had planned to study English literature – because her mother had said she should. After three weeks she had felt this to be a complete waste of time. Instead she changed to theatre arts with the intention of becoming a scenic designer, but two months later she realised that what really interested her in theatre was the people and why they behaved the way they did. She had also read Freud for years and became so fascinated by neurotic behaviour that she decided to study psychology.

"But in the study of behaviour it still eluded me why people suffer. Why does one person come to life burdened with one situation and another with another? There had to be some kind of order behind it, which psychology couldn't give me. I had lost my belief in orthodox religion, yet believed in something that had purpose. I couldn't put the two together until astrology began to do it for me. A reason why one person had one kind of life and another another; some kind of purpose behind it.

"I realised what rubbish a lot of 'straight' psychology was when I saw a particularly obnoxious Freudian analyst as part of my training. It was a very unpleasant encounter. Many of the ideas made sense but it had no soul in it, no love of people. People were reduced to something between a salivating dog and a rat in a machine. I was horrified because I knew intuitively that psychology was desperately important.

Nobody knew how to do anything with it, nobody was helping anyone with it. Obviously there are good Freudian analysts who occupy an important place, but it depends on the analysist, not the theory. If a person is whole inside, he will heal. It made me realise what lack of respect for the dignity of the human being there was in academic psychology. In astrology I saw the connection between the individual and the cosmos. It flipped me out. I thought, the psychologists don't realise, this provides a universal perspective."

Then, on top of this experience, a month or two later she learned about reincarnation and suddenly everything became clear. As a child, Liz had believed in reincarnation without understanding what it was. She was convinced that she had been alive during the height of the Egyptian civilisation around 2000 BC, and also during the Renaissance. It was just an absolute certainty although she had never told this to anyone.

"And then for the first time I heard a philosophic system put forward which included the idea of karma, of personal destiny, and the interrelationships between people and the development of the soul. All very theosophic but it didn't matter. Everything knit together; my own breakdown, my training and the realization that I had chosen my parents because I had to put myself in this situation. Everything became full of meaning, imbued with a sense of the existence of some intelligence, of a god-like principle within human beings that could act as a guide through life."

This awakening came to Liz at a meeting in a friend's flat, but half-way through she had to get up. She went to the bathroom and cried and cried with sheer release. When she came back into the room people asked what had happened to her, she looked completely different. She had wiped away the traces of crying and looked as usual but her face had completely changed. She couldn't tell them. She couldn't talk to anyone.

"What burst through was the meaning of what my life would be. But I knew too that there was no way my emotional, physical and intellectual nature could have understood it because everything was a mess. I had so much personality damage, particularly on the emotional level; I was full of all kinds of negative patterns which took me the next ten years to deal with. I am just beginning to live the meaning of that experience. It has taken the ten years in between to get my twisted wreck into some sort of human shape so it could carry a little bit of that; to be able to live it as a reality on an individual, personal, feeling level instead of some spiritual recognition.

"The turning point came at nineteen. I knew I had something to do and that somewhere it would have meaning. I had no idea what it was, but after that experience I knew that everyone's life must mean something and take a wholly individual path. I made a commitment. I went through a religious conversion in the sense that I committed myself to be of service to this sense."

LORRAINE GILL at thirty-six is an accomplished artist, a painter. She is now a strong, worldly woman with an infectious laugh, but there was little in her early life to laugh about. "I hated my father, he was often drunk and brutal. Now I understand his frustrations, but at the time I used to lie in bed thinking how to kill him. He was a total dictator and unless we were out of the house we had no respite from tension. He used to beat my mother and one time drenched her with a pot of boiling water which scarred her chest for life. As a child, I used to watch the planes fly out of Australia into the sunset and I was totally certain there had to be another and a better place. I had a secret boyfriend at fifteen. He asked me to marry him but he had to be joking. I'd got things to do and places to go."

Lorraine's father was a car salesman. Her mother read romances and he read nothing at all. But for some reason, she says, she became quite good at school. She was fascinated by Florentine culture and medieval history and books on the Renaissance somehow gravitated towards her. It seemed inexplicable at the time but later it made sense. Encouraged by a sympathetic art teacher she went, at fifteen, to the biggest art school in Sydney. "I was a country bumpkin. I had never been in such a stable environment, a place where people behaved normally. The first day I tripped over my feet and dropped things in sheer terror,"

She made a friend who became her mentor, and for the first time she told someone about her home life; before she had been too ashamed. "When I got depressed my friend talked about the rhythms of life and said that God was watching over me. I wondered where He was and why He allowed my family to go through what they did. I felt different, but not quite sure if it was because of my background. I was very naive compared to the rest of my friends, a child. And I was never in the swing of things."

The friend she trusted pleaded with the authorities to get Lorraine away from home and at nineteen, six months before the end of college, she left home without a backward glance. To support herself she worked in the evenings as a telephonist. By the end of college, commercial art had become too assembly-line for Lorraine; she knew she couldn't create in that environment. "My energies had been so inhibited at home that they had to be transferred to something else. That's why I took up dancing. I was an inherently violent person and felt I needed a physical way of releasing tension."

By chance she saw a Spanish dance team on television and this seemed the right thing to do, to balance herself out. She found a Spanish classical dance teacher and was determined to work hard at that. "I went to live with the woman, and because I was working so hard I became her protégé. I performed in public and featured in the newspapers, but then her husband caused trouble. Because I wouldn't sleep with him he told her that I had, and I was thrown out bag and baggage because she didn't believe me."

Still working as a telephonist at night, she found herself a place to live next to Sydney harbour. This was the first time that she had been in an environment with trees and sea and ferry boats. She was happy just to watch the stars and play music whenever she wanted to. "It was the first time I had experienced my own company and I liked it."

Over the next six months she went through one set of

bizarre experiences after another. She met a Dutch boy who played the guitar and went to live with his family in Adelaide, but was soon thrown out after a contrived argument about etiquette. She pawned her jewellery for the bus fare back to Sydney and met a doctor on the bus who later asked her to marry him. A warning bell said 'no' and afterwards she learned he was a con-man performing minor operations in big hospitals all over the country, before he was discovered. She finally went back to her home at the harbour and found herself another Spanish dance teacher who could teach her Flamenco. He suggested she should go to Spain and "one morning I woke up knowing I was going."

She went to stay with her grandmother to begin to save some money. She took one job in an art shop during the day and another giving ballroom dancing lessons in the evenings. At weekends she painted a mural for the Arthur Murray studio. "I grew to love my grandmother; she was totally loyal, stable and loving. My dad had disowned me. When I left my grandmother, she wept her heart out."

With her bank book and nowhere certain to go, she took a boat to Spain. She walked around Madrid until through her limited Spanish she found a Spanish dance teacher "a little dark woman like an overgrown frog", in an underground labyrinth. The physical discipline was tremendous. She learned ten dances in eighteen months, but although her Flamenco was excellent she could not perform the ballet sections required at the auditions. Without a job, no work permit and no money she had to leave. On her way back to Australia she came to England and in a room in Islington she had a premonition that something was wrong. Her uncle wrote to tell her that her grandmother had committed suicide and there was no point in her coming home. "Everything had gone and I was in total desolation."

At this time she met Tony. "He was the first person who understood that I was not particularly good with words. My whole life had been spent in survival and physical discipline. He would say 'do you know what that means?', and I said no. I had the understanding but I couldn't express it. I didn't even know that the sun was the centre of the solar system. My ignorance was almost total. He took me in and in the next three years, until I was twenty-eight, he taught me the power of articulation and the use of words. But I felt every string that attached me to reality had been cut. I didn't want to live, I was tired out. I also felt a burden to Tony because I thought my life was totally useless."

At one time Tony was ill in hospital and Lorraine took him some spontaneous, impromptu drawings to cheer him up. Immediately he told her she must go back to art college. "He literally took me there and forced me. I went to Camden Art Centre in the evenings and one of the teachers recommended me for a grant."

But in her intense pain and insecurity she was constantly trying to undermine Tony. "It was a love-hate relationship. I hated him because of his inner happiness and optimism and cleverness. I tried to bring him down to my level, to break him down."

When she had almost succeeded, she realised that no person has the right to use emotional blackmail or to cause this kind of destruction. So she left. "I found an attic in Clapham Road and began working like a fanatic. I wanted to know the why about everything and no one could answer my questions, so I took the personal responsibility of finding out. Even as a child I wanted to understand why there was so much suffering and degradation and ignorance. I wanted to find out how life worked. I began to find strength by being alone, and through the encouragement of my work. And then I happened to see a book by John Berger."

By this time she was gaining a reputation in the art school and decided to write to him because she wanted some answers to her questions. He came to see her. "He was extremely kind to me. It was the first time I had ever met a man who could relate to the feminine side of my nature. He talked to me about making paintings without political motives, but purely for the sake of nature and discovering new forms. I discovered a man whose vast experience of reading paintings was totally in tune with what I felt. He showed me how looking at painting could be part of life, part of education, a way of achieving dignity and value as a human being – and need not be materially oriented. He grounded all the intuitive feelings I had ever had."

At the art college, her Principal had become a wonderful friend and Lorraine flourished. She won a scholarship and spent three weeks in Florence. "I had been thinking of the meaningless state of painting in England; of its aggression and lack of feeling for the beauty in life. But in Florence I saw and felt the achievement of human beings; many human beings, because there were so many works of art."

And she saw the Michelangelo David. "Tourists were rushing around clicking their cameras and then rushing back out. They had no idea of their own relationship to history, in terms of what men can achieve. History was simply taken for granted; they didn't identify with it. I sat in a corner and wept, suddenly aware of what an individual could achieve, given the will and direction. It was totally over-powering. I was completely overwhelmed by the potential of the human species, and I looked at humanity with a growing love because of the beauty of this single work, a magnificent victory of life over death.

"I wasn't set on my path in terms of my work, but I knew then what it was possible for me to do."

LYNICE YATES is thirty, a class teacher at the Bristol Waldorf School – where education is based on the teachings of Rudolf Steiner. She is a solid, competent person, coming forward now only with some reluctance, and yet so dedicated when she does commit herself, that she is at the moment totally involved in taking one class of children through the entire first eight years of their education. Born in Morecambe, Lancashire, she felt left out of things at twelve. Painfully shy, she was always part of the out-crowd. "Yet I felt it unjustified, because outside wasn't my place. I used to feel so strongly different from other children; I knew I was going to do something different with my life, because there was something else in the world."

She was good at school, one of the top of the class, but a difficult student. "I was pushed intellectually at school, although I didn't realise it at the time. At home there was no cultural life, nothing that could awaken me to the beauty of life through the arts. I suppose I sensed I wasn't getting what I needed as an individual, and kicked out."

Liverpool University at eighteen was fun for the first year, but then she grew bored. A job seemed dreary too. At twenty she caught the wander-lust and, since she was studying for a degree in French, she hitch-hiked with a friend to France.

"That changed my whole life. The best thing was meeting a whole new culture. The French were very different. Unlike my British student friends, they did a lot of questioning about life. I met communists, anarchists, Trotskyists and all the other 'ists' who confronted me with things I had never thought about before. Then during the second year I hitch-hiked all round Europe with virtually no money, just living from day to day and roughing it. I came across the real down and outs, the whole hippy culture, the really sordid part of life. I met Paris drug addicts, homosexuals, tramps; everyone living that sort of life. Being with people with nothing at all made me question everything about life and society."

Her third major experience was an inner one. She met Jean-Pierre who has perhaps been the most important influence in her life. "We met at a party and just looked at each other. It was as though we had known each other before. He was interested in Buddhism and Eastern religion and through him I read some rather silly books by Lobsang Rampa, but which in a way were quite good; about a man who claimed to be a Tibetan monk and had taken the body of an Englishman to try to bring his knowledge to the West. He talked a great deal about reincarnation and meditation, and in simple down-to-earth terms compared all spiritual forces to electricity. I find it rather materialistic now, but it took something logical and rational to interest me. I couldn't dispute these things and when I read about them they seemed so obvious. Why hadn't anyone told me all this before? It seemed the most obvious solution to life."

That year she went with Jean-Pierre to Aix-en-Provence where finally she took her degree. It was a year in which she met a number of people doing strange things: psychic healers, astrologers, members of the Rosicrucian movement. "It was a significant year because I was bombarded with these things." She couldn't shut her eyes. Ultimately they went to Morocco and then she returned to Liverpool.

"But within two weeks I knew I couldn't go back to that meaningless life. All my friends were thinking of going into dreadful jobs because 'the money was good'. I knew I couldn't do that with my life."

She was in a dilemma. Jean-Pierre sent telegrams begging her to come back to France, and an English boyfriend asked her to marry him. England would mean security with someone who loved her. Jean-Pierre would never mean that, but life would be exciting and alive. "I know subconsciously I was given a choice; to sink into security and conform or go forging ahead."

She returned to France and was totally miserable. They lived in a crazy, crowded flat in dreadful conditions. She was lonely because she had no friends and depended on Jean-Pierre. "But I knew what I was doing, I had chosen to make these things happen."

When Jean-Pierre inherited some land in Corsica he talked about setting up a community there. "And one night I had a dream about Corsica, a very idyllic dream. From then on I knew I would go there. Our relationship was very bad and actually came to an end during that time, but I would not give up the idea of going to Corsica because it was such a strong certainty. Something inside me said it was important to go."

She went to Corsica at twenty-three and the two years she spent there turned her completely inside out. At first there were six in the group living in hopeless conditions with virtually no money. Living as peasants, growing vegetables, rearing goats and hens and collecting olives to make oil, they did not know quite what it was they were doing, but they believed in it absolutely.

As time went on the vague ideals grew more concrete but the life wasn't easy. A very lonely group in the middle of an alien culture. They tried to develop some sort of spiritual life but here again they did not know where they were going or what they were doing. "For me there was great conflict," says Lynice. "I was involved in the Rosicrucian idea but it was completely intellectual. When it came to doing things like fasting or meditating or anything which involved working inwardly, I wasn't interested – although I knew somehow it was right. My problem was that I was trying to follow what other people were doing and it went against the grain of something in me. I felt guilty because I knew it was right to have a spiritual life, but I didn't have my own place in it."

But more than this, living in a community you learn to see yourself face to face, and she found this extremely painful. She was seeking self-knowledge and began to discover things about herself which she did not like. She hated people not to like her and was trying to change herself. "Living in Corsica made me unhappy and a thoroughly horrible person, as we all could be. It was partly material conditions. We didn't have enough food and of course this makes people selfish and pick on each other. We were living too closely together and for a whole year I was the only female in the community which was also difficult. I was more emotional than the others. They were steady in themselves but I had a lot of questions about myself. Also I didn't quite know why I was there and was in terrible conflict about whether to stay or leave. For a long time I couldn't leave because I had nowhere to go. I also stayed out of wilfulness. I couldn't go back and have everyone say 'I told you so'. For this reason I went through a lot which anyone else would have walked out on. It was a mixture of will and fear and rightness."

At the end of two years someone came along and talked about Rudolf Steiner. "It was the first time I had heard the spiritual life connected with the practical life around us. I had always found it difficult to sit down and meditate and relate to 'cosmic space' with no practical consequences. But Steiner gave a picture of man as a spiritual reality, as a being who existed before birth and who continues to exist after death. He gave a clear picture of reincarnation and said that everyone was on earth in order to grow. This made sense to me."

Then something equally important happened' Lynice was twenty-five when she took one, and only one, trip on the drug LSD – and this proved to be a major turning point in her life. "I had been reading a lot about psychic experiences on LSD but had never had the courage to take it. I knew that being emotionally insecure, it was not a good idea. I had been given this one dose by a friend and I kept it for a long time. I thought I should use it only if the circumstances were absolutely right."

By a string of strange coincidences a friend turned up in Corsica and one day during his visit she felt it right to take it with him. "I took it because of the conflict between my intellect and my inner being. Intellectually I knew there was a spiritual world, but I didn't *know* it. I was sitting on a gate refusing to step forward. If I took it I knew I would know the answer and I knew I wouldn't be able to go back. It was a strong and positive experience."

Looking back she realised that she had had vague psychic experiences before, although she hadn't been sure. She could see that being in Corsica itself had done something to her. The power of the island had affected her. She was aware of this to a degree. She had also been aware since living in France that the physical world wasn't the ultimate reality, but one only very dimly perceived. "Once I understood the whole idea of destiny and karma and reincarnation I suddenly saw my whole life in a different way. I saw that everything that had happened; the people I had met, the way my life had gone and the way I saw myself were all part of a vast pattern, and the more that pattern wove in incredible ways, the more I knew my life wasn't mere chance. Of course I was free to take the situations that came, and could act in freedom, but those things were meant to happen. This was a startling revelation to me and changed my whole life. It taught me to accept – and I'm still learning – everything that happens to me and not to judge it in itself, because in a few years it will appear as part of that pattern and seem quite different."

Suddenly she knew she must go into education although she wasn't sure how or when.

Isobel McGilvray is thirty-six and practises her own version of the Alexander Technique therapy. She is very blonde, very gentle and serene and calls her work 'balancing' rather than healing. Born on an isolated farm in New Zealand, Isobel says she has almost always had a sense that there was a path which some part of her was laying down before her. A sense of her life as a pattern; not predestined but presenting a certain course which she was going to follow. Until more recently there were times when it seemed almost out of her hands.

Her isolation and closeness to the earth were, she feels, valuable roots and continue to provide a link with the rightness of that path. The things that triggered her to new directions came into her life like signposts; almost logical happenings taking place at precise moments so she wouldn't lose her way. "There was tremendous pressure on everyone to conform, but as far as I can remember I knew there had to be other ways. Who was to say that we were right? But my spontaneity and creativity were very repressed and I conformed."

For several years she went through a religious phase during which she wanted to be a missionary and administer to "the poor primitive people who didn't know better!" At seventeen she began nursing. "It was a shock. Until then I had lived in isolation. Here I was faced with people whose problems were very real, and all my high-falutin' religious ideas didn't mean anything to them."

Even then, although her thinking was orthodox, she queried everything everyone said, especiallly about patients who didn't fit easily into any of the usual medical categories. "And I realised that every time I was ill myself the solution wasn't in the text books. I just got better by myself. I realised there was something very screwy going on, and that is when I really started doubting that theirs was the only way of looking at things. I knew there had to be better ways of healing people."

From the age of seventeen she had completely thrown herself into nursing, but there came a time when she realised she had left no life for herself. She had no doubts about her mental and professional abilities, but she had no idea about being a person. And she was also questioning the extensive use of drugs and surgery; and the lack of humanity in medicine. She had pushed herself to physical, mental and emotional exhaustion, so she made up her mind to leave. She spent three months at home doing nothing, and then went into private nursing. "Decisions have never been a problem because I have always had this sense of knowing when something I was doing was absolutely right. I know this was all trying to come through very much. I packed my things in my car and for the first time my life wasn't planned or organised, which I knew for me was quite important. At twenty-five I set myself loose, and I didn't know where I was going."

She went to Wellington. "I had looked at things like colour healing and astrology and thought they were peculiar, but when these ideas were presented to me again by the daughter of an elderly patient of mine, I was prepared to listen. I respected her because she was a practising Christian which in my terms was relatively important, although I had given up religion myself. I didn't feel she was a crank. Perhaps there was something in it. Some time later I put my back out and went to a chiropractor. This really was crank country, but I wasn't going to a doctor because I knew he couldn't help me.

"Then I began doing palmistry and discovered I was quite good at it. I wouldn't have done it at all except I bought this book for my sister-in-law and read it before I sent it to her. At first it was just fun trying to read my friends' hands, but then I started being impressed with what I saw."

This is when Isobel began to develop the intuitive ability which had already come through in her nursing. People used to call her "X-ray Eyes" because she could always distinguish between those who were really ill and those who were dissembling. "I didn't question it too much. In a sense that part of me didn't want to realise it was important. I didn't question how it might happen, but I could see things coming through a little bit more; almost see patterns emerging."

At twenty-seven she made up her mind to come to

England, where she spent a very unhappy eighteen months. As she says, for her there was never any trouble finding the path, but being on it was often hard work. "I was really cut off from everything and I hadn't realised how big a part roles had played in my life; as a prefect at the local school, as a sister in the hospital. For the first time I knew nobody and was completely free to be myself."

It was a lonely and difficult time because she had no idea who she was dealing with. Until a very large signpost appeared. "Before I left New Zealand I had seen a photograph of the son of a woman patient. Immediately I had the feeling that I had to meet him. I had this strong sense that this man was meant for me. I don't know how to describe it, but when we did meet over here, I felt that he felt it too; yet neither of us could cope with it. In fact I only had a drink with him, a matter of three hours, and never saw him again. It was an important trigger and I don't understand how it works, but now I believe we had known each other in a previous life. I felt literally as though something had hit me in the solar plexus and I couldn't get my breath.

"I came from a very rural background with a lousy education and I suffered because I felt I should have had a better one. I didn't know about the arts or anything. He was from a sophisticated family with a good education and knew all about things. Somehow he saw in me the person I am now; what I wasn't then. It upset me and made me aware of what I wasn't.

"I think I began developing all those bits in myself. I didn't like myself basically and I think I began to develop awareness of other bits of myself. He started my mind in a totally different direction. My taste in just about everything changed, I was so affected by this man. I went into a great depression and was quite suicidal. I felt that the purpose of my life was to be with him, and if I couldn't then there was no purpose.

"Obviously I needed a shock to shift my whole way of thinking. I couldn't understand it on any level I knew. There was no guidance, nobody to point me in any direction. I was in complete desolation with no one to talk it over with, but I began to find myself walking along the street aware I was seeing things totally differently."

During these eighteen months she also had two major psychic experiences. On a visit to her aunt in Scotland she saw her uncle who had been dead for six months. He was sitting in a chair that wasn't there and smoking a pipe. "In the morning I almost talked myself out of it, but the interesting thing is that I wasn't surprised. I seemed to take it for granted, except my mind was freaking out in the middle of it!"

At the same time she was working in a hospital where there were reports of ghosts; including one particularly bad one who tried to choke nurses on night duty. "I was attacked by this thing one night and it was a terrifying experience. I woke up and could feel these hands on my throat, a feeling of total evil, not just a person. I knew there was nothing to see and was terrified. My reaction was to say 'what's the matter, what do you want?' We had it exorcised and after a few more times it seemed to get weaker."

This period of eighteen months was like a prolonged gestation. As though she were trying to give birth but the moment was not quite right. "I realised changes were going on and felt great frustration. I didn't really want to be in nursing and my back was giving me a lot of trouble."

Then the barrier seemed to lift and she got a job on a health farm where she could favour her back with lighter work. There, at Tyringham in Buckinghamshire, she was introduced to many kinds of alternative healing and medicine. "My sceptical mind tended to question, but I tried to be open and it did change my thinking.

"Up to then I had a knowing that I was knowing, but not knowing. If I tuned in I knew, but my logical mind didn't want to. I wasn't quite into it myself, but I was interested in learning everything. I came into contact first with the better-known accepted techniques like acupuncture, massage, osteopathy and herbal medicine."

And it was here that at twenty-eight she had her first peak experience. One day she joined a relaxation class taken by one of her colleagues. Through hypnosis he was taking the class back to a closeness with the mother and with the earth. "I really did have the experience of limitlessness and of becoming one with the universe; where I felt that the trees, the grass, the sky, the world and I were one. A sense of waking to the experience that there were no definite boundaries, no edges to my body. It was a major turning point for me."

Soon afterwards she was introduced to the Alexander Technique. She had just met the important man of her life and he had recommended it for her back. "He told me 'this is what you'll want to do'. And after the first ten minutes of my lesson I knew this was exactly what I wanted to do, that I couldn't go wrong. It was a big decision, but on the other hand I knew the decision had already been made. I'd simply been searching out the means."

DIANA BECCHETTI is thirty-one and works as a counsellor in Psychosynthesis. She is a dark-eyed, loving lady; the good fairy at the christening. "When I was seven I thought I was alive to make other people happy, especially my family because then they were my whole universe. They were very unhappy, all of them; my parents and my two brothers. For years when I went to bed at night I said my prayers and asked God to give me my family's pain. I'm sure some of the pain I've been through is related to this. It worked. I was able to make them smile when they were miserable. It was incredible. I could laugh them out of depression. There was a sense that I didn't matter very much. Not in a self-negating way, just that I was not the major focus. I've been fighting to cut the umbilical cord ever since."

But not until she reached adolescence did Diana realise she was unhappy. From a small mid-West American farming community, a stable middle-class environment for a child to grow up, with little crime and no danger in being alone, she was given a typical American education. After high-school 12th grade she took a year off to work, "which I didn't like, so at twenty university was the answer how not to work."

When she was twenty-one, a girlfriend on campus decided to drop out for the winter and be a ski-bum in Aspen,

Colorado. The night before she left Diana decided to go too. "I'd never left home before; I was still a virgin and had never taken drugs. That winter changed all three of those things. I discovered drugs, sex and a very different way of life."

For the next four years she dropped out every other quarter to go to the mountains. She lived in two worlds. She couldn't give up one world completely to go to the other, she was too frightened. She went to the mountains to be a ski-bum, take drugs and be with nature, and then she would go back to her courses in advertising and public relations. "It sounds a very sleazy time. In the mountains I spent a lot of time alone, getting high and reconnecting to nature as I hadn't done since I was a child. The only time I was really happy was with nature. I couldn't cope with relationships and I had no aims. It was very therapeutic going back to find myself, but I couldn't do it completely. I felt like Walter Mitty. At college, where I also worked as a model and a modelling teacher, I was this synthetic fashion-model type person wearing false eyelashes. And in the mountains I was this freak living a seemingly organic existence, except for the drugs. I see it as a period of trying to find myself. Having lived most of my life for other peope I suddenly became hedonistic and said 'now it's my turn.' I went crazy in the mountains and only worked, as a cocktail waitress, when I needed money."

At twenty-five a boyfriend gave Diana a book called *Joy* by William Schutz, the father of encounter groups in the States. It was like reading about another world, another planet. The book was about the human potential movement, about people and how out of touch we are with our emotions. She knew she had to go to Esalen to seen what it was about.

Esalen was founded originally as a small community on the beautiful Big Sur coast by Dick Price and Michael Murphy, but eventually it became a centre which practised Gestalt therapy and Humanistic psychology. These are techniques which delve into the emotions and deal with them, not mentally, but experientially, most often by producing a catharsis or discharge of emotion which bring unconscious problems to conscious attention.

"I went to Esalen for a week and everything changed. I was

forced inside myself to understand the outside, and I didn't like what I saw at all. It was frightening on every level." In a five-day Gestalt workshop she looked at different parts of herself, taking them out and 'becoming them'. "The frustrating thing was that I saw I was a very superficial person who had never done anything meaningful with my life. I had never been a real person as I defined it. I wasn't open and honest with people and not willing to admit weaknesses. I saw my faults very clearly that week. It was exquisite to find that I could do something about myself. I wasn't the victim of an unfortunate background. I could no longer blame my family life for being in a mess. I was responsible for who I was. I could say I'm doing it myself and take responsibility for that. I saw I could change."

These experiences were both positive and negative; they were totally traumatic with great heights of enthusiasm and depths of despair. They were frustrating and exciting. She was frightened because she knew it was the biggest step forward of her life. She knew strongly that there was something here that was right for her. She could never go back to her other life. She had to explore. "I didn't know anything more specific than that," she says. "But I felt I would never be the same after that experience."

After three months at home she knew there was no turning back. She had to move forward. It was a moment of choice. "But it was almost as if in the moment I made that choice, I was given tremendous energy to break up with an old boyfriend who wanted to marry me, to leave my father and make my own life. I couldn't stay in the other world and knew I had to find myself consciously now before I could do anything else. I didn't know where I was going or who I was. I had chosen before to drop out in the mountains and be a hippy, but I hadn't known then what a hippy was. I knew it was something about peace and love and nature and loving people instead of fighting them. But later I found it was a big sham. I soon grew disillusioned with those people, they were just as distorted as the conventional world, playing destructive games. I think it started out as a good thing, but people messed it up. I'd tried both worlds and neither was what I was looking for. Esalen was another attempt at a third kind of world. Maybe this was what I was looking for."

Back at Esalen, her insecurity was so bad she felt that people would run from her if they knew what she was really like. Relating back to the modelling days, she felt that for all those years she had worn a shell and had never developed inside, she was empty. She threw herself into the growth process. She had wasted twenty-five years and had to make up for them. After a year Dick Price told her that he felt she had potential and would like to train her. "It was a tremendous shock that someone wanted to train *me*." She studied as an apprentice for almost two years, learning totally by experience, and began leading groups. They were very intense times with great leaps forward. It was here she met John when he came to make a film and she left Esalen to live with him at the beginning of a budding career when everything was going for her. "It amazes me when I look back, but although I didn't love him there was no question that I had to go."

Within three months at John's home in the Bahamas, they fell in love. But they knew they couldn't stay and because Diana knew she needed more credentials they went back to Santa Barbara for her to take her Master's degree in Confluent Education. At Esalen it had been a case of helping people in their psychological lives. Now she became more conscious of the spiritual nature of her path.

It was in Santa Barbara that she and John were introduced to the spiritual world by 'crazy man' Jim Hurtak, Professor of Oriental Studies, philosopher and Rabbi, who claimed he had been consciously taken to another planet. "He became our teacher for three horrific, intense months. He took us on field trips to the tops of mountains looking for UFOs and taught us ridiculous Jewish chants which made us laugh. Nothing else happened. His class ended up with eight hours a week of teaching on the Bible. We couldn't understand a word he was saying but no one wanted to admit it. It was a powerful initiation and for me horrific. I spent most of the time in chaos. He took our ego boundaries and blasted them. When you haven't thought about these things, it is quite a shock."

It was here, too, that she discovered Psychosynthesis, a new form of psychology founded by an Italian doctor, Roberto Assagioli, which takes man's spiritual nature into consideration as well as the psychological. "I thought it was just another trick for my tool bag," she says. "I didn't take it very seriously even after the basic training. But then we came to Europe and decided for many silly reasons, like the fact that I was Italian, to go and see Assagioli.

"Immediately I saw him I had a real feeling of just coming home. There was an energy and vibration about him on another level. It was a tremendously emotional exprience and we were like old friends from the beginning. I knew him like from a hundred past lives. I knew I was in the presence of a very high being, a great man. He was radiant and with that radiance was the most incredible joy. Joy like the light from a lighthouse came out of him, and when you were with him he could put you in touch with that part of you, so you were joyful. He had a way of zapping you vibrationally. And at this point I *knew*. I knew this was my life's work. I interpreted it as psychosynthesis but now I see it as 'service'."

These, then, are the five visible threads in my pattern. Five women of my acquaintance who have each experienced some form of personal call, who have been imbued in some way with an element of wisdom.

Each of them has chosen a different path. And while I do not necessarily agree with any of their methods or their philosophies, or they with mine, I do believe that all their paths lead through initiation and growth to the same goal of awareness and fulfillment. And, for this reason alone, are worth exploring.

Where there's a Will

*"The terrible thing about life
is that wanting, longing, has
been eliminated from people;
or if they do want, they don't
know what they want."*

Laurens Van der Post in *Vogue,* January 1977

No parents get it right in bringing up their children. They are either too strict or too free; too cold or too loving; too poor or too rich. Whichever way they play it, we manage to blame them for something that goes wrong in our lives. Everyone has their pain, even in a peaceful house. The pain is relative. For Liz the pain was in relationships. She desperately wanted to love and be loved, to have an emotional rapport with someone so she didn't feel so completely cut off, but every relationship she had fell to pieces. For Diana the basic problem of insecurity and lack of confidence came up. in whatever aspect of herself she was working on. It was always this same pattern; she was trying to like herself.

Any growth is painful. And one of the prerequisites, it seems, is not to have the kind of ready-made support from parents that the so-called healthy child has. Then we are forced to find something on our own. We have to have a glimpse of things other than those that satisfy the senses. If we cannot imagine there could be something else, we are stuck. It is the perception of more, and the pain caused by the gap that this perception brings, that makes us move. It instigates a feeling of longing, the need for something more. Lynice was striving for perfection and finding herself imperfect. Isobel disliked herself as a teenager, and becoming a Christian gave her a reason for not liking herself. Hers became a journey for God and gave her a purpose in life, which carried her through adolescence. When she took up nursing she was once again covered by a role. She didn't quite have to face the fact that she didn't like herself. For a long time she didn't allow herself to look at things too closely, but when she came to London and was no longer able to hide behind her professional role, she had to find out who she was.

For some people the rigours of life don't weigh so heavily and the need to move lies dormant. But for many, their background, whatever that may be, presents a pattern of behaviour with which they simply cannot gel. When the wrongness becomes so acute that pain builds to traumatic levels, something has to break. In order to survive, there has to be a way of finding new aspects in ourselves. The sense of insecurity and inadequacy sets off an overwhelming motivation to grow and change. We have to go out to find, and then to learn to like ourselves. Lorraine, in whatever situation she found herself, always felt intellectually inferior. Because she could never express herself adequately, she was never listened to, she was *persona non grata*. She knew she had to have the word power to articulate what she knew inside, before anyone would take her seriously. It seemed she was being propelled from one situation to another with incredible struggles from day to day. She had to survive at all costs.

In such circumstances the Will is forced into action. How the power of the Will awakens is difficult to describe except by paths to it. When you want or need something desperately you do things that help that want. And suddenly what you are doing becomes part of you. Roberto Assagioli said "The Will exists. We have a Will and we are our Will." When you realise this, you realise you can change yourself. You can choose. By using the Will consciously you can change your personality and circumstances. The Will, which Assagioli called the Cinderella of psychology, holds untold magic. It is an incredibly dynamic concept.

A Strong Will is not enough. 'My Will be done' in the Victorian sense implies power and suppression. What we need is, as Assagioli put it, a 'Skillful Will', so that we "set in motion the parts of ourselves that already have the tendency to produce the specific things we are aiming for." Used in an artistic way we get the most done with the least amount of energy expended. Once we realise a need or a hope, the Will (and at this stage it is our 'Personal Will') automatically sets itself into motion. Our Will must also be a 'Good Will', which Assagioli explained through the two laws of physics and psychology: 'The Law of Action and Reaction' and 'The Law of Rhythm and Equilibrium'. These laws say that those who cause harm, attract harm upon themselves; those who are violent and merciless, in the end bring the violence and cruelty of others against themselves. So the Will, to be effective, must be good; good towards ourselves and towards others.

"Every idea is an act at an initial stage", said William James; a concept reinforced by Assagioli. If you concentrate on an idea or imagine yourself doing something you want to do, this, he said, tends to produce the actual action needed to do it. If you imagine yourself to be confident in a certain situation, the confidence tends to come. The Will can also physically set the energies of your imagination and thought in motion, so you can carry out your idea. It will automatically trigger the minute muscular action necessary to begin the job. A small exercise indicates this. Tie to a thin stick a piece of string with a bead on one end. Dangle it over the centre of a large circle drawn on a sheet of paper. Without moving the stick, by moving your eyes round and round, imagine the bead moving around the circumference of the circle. The bead will gradually begin to swing around that circle without you moving the stick. Very weird! But it isn't quite magic. You can't feel you are moving the stick but as you 'will' the wand to move, in fact you set up an imperceptible muscular movement of the hand. The image in your mind has a motor effect.

Again, if you 'act as if' and pretend to be something or do something, this too can bring on the actual feeling that you have adopted for the part. If you raise your voice and pretend to be angry, you find that you really do begin to feel angry. A group of people did a relevant experiment in which one half pretended to be prisoners and the other half pretended to be warders. They acted out a pertinent scene. By the end of the experiment the warders had taken on the actions of prison warders and were treating the 'prisoners' in a cruel and menacing way.

What we imagine, we become. If, for example, you are desperately miserable because you feel you have no intellect, you might force yourself to read books and newspapers that seem way above your head. But after much perseverence and worry about being a fraud, you will suddenly discover that these books really are of interest to you. If you dare to throw in an opinion or two from these books, gradually you will realise that you are adapting these to genuine ones of your own. Any image has the tendency to transform itself on the physical plane. Energy follows thought. "As you think, so shall you become."

The Will can obviously work in a negative way. Emotions can trigger happenings that correspond to those feelings. If you worry constantly about being ill, you begin to imagine all kinds of illnesses and these mental pictures will tend to produce the physical symptoms that go with them. This happens a great deal in psychosomatic illness.

But this knowledge about the Will can be used in a positive way. Two American basketball teams were in training. One trained physically in the usual way, but the other trained in their imaginations and, implausible as it appears, those trained in their imagination actually played better. To give another example, if you are asked to think of words beginning with the letter C, they keep popping into your mind for a long time afterwards. The unconcious keeps the energy going. It is a mysterious relationship between the psychological and the physical. When we want to bend a knee we are not aware of the complex mechanism involved, we just bend it. And it is the same for everything in the psyche. A mental picture begins activity in the unconscious towards its fulfillment. If you adopt a positive image, if you build an image of yourself as a growing, moving person this image will become a reality. We can deprogramme ourselves from the things we don't like and set a new programme.

If we want to do something badly enough we can do it. If it is a fight for survival, we have to succeed. The Will begins to work because it has to, as it did for these women. The need was to establish the 'I', the ego, and at that stage the personal will was endeavouring to find a likeable, acceptable personality of its own. There was an overwhelming motivation to grow. In order to survive, they had to find new places within themselves.

Motivation or Will is the key to the growth process. A modest ability with strong motivation really does achieve more than a great talent with lesser motivation. Once you have chosen or been forced by circumstances to set the Will in motion, it continues to function; it automatically becomes part of your Will to Life. But the Will does not stop at the personal will. Our needs do not stop at our personal needs. In fact we all have what Abraham Maslow called a 'hierarchy of human needs'. Once we have satisfied more or less unconsciously, our physical need for food and shelter, for order and security in our lives, we move on to a need for love and a sense of belonging and a need for esteem, from ourselves and others. When these needs have been fulfilled we move on again to a need for expression of our own nature. Maslow called this need for achievement in the things we have chosen to do "self-actualisation".

If we become muddled and find ourselves unable to cope during this upward growth towards self-actualisation, we can turn for help to psychology. In the old days, psychology promised us magic; a study of the mind that would resolve our confusions and problems and help us to adapt satisfactorily to our surroundings.

The first force in psychology, which dominated until the mid-19th century, was Behaviourist Psychology. It was philosophical and experimental. Psychology was taken to the laboratory and every idea had to be proved on a scientific

41

basis. As Pavlov conditioned his dogs to behave in a certain manner, so it was believed that a man, with the right sort of conditioning, could be made a good and useful member of society. Man, in other words, was a "bundle of manageable reactions."

The second force in psychology, at the other end of the scale, was the Psychoanalytical, brought to prominence by Freud. By exploring the elements of the unconscious in the psyche and clearing out all the rubbish accumulated since childhood, the psychoanalyst made an attempt to remove the obstacles to our happiness which would help us to adjust to the society we lived in. These were therapies which looked primarily at mental problems and breakdowns and quite obviously do have their place.

The third force is Humanistic Psychology which integrates the psychological needs of the individual and helps him to self-actualisation. It deals with sensitivity training, but has tended towards emotionally oriented gatherings; such as Encounter Groups and Transactional Analysis Groups which go into the emotions experientially, to release blockages to growth and self-actualisation. These can be useful therapies, but they seldom go far enough. All too often they become excuses for "emotional masturbation", vehicles for dumping one's emotional rubbish on other people.

But happily, the satisfaction of achieving for oneself seldom lasts. For many people it brings boredom, emptiness and meaninglessness; a feeling of personal futility because life has no point. So the Will continues on its path towards a Will to Meaning. And our need grows into a 'transpersonal need'; a concern with something broader than the mere individual. The need to believe that we live in a meaningful universe. And this need has brought with it a new kind of psychology. The sort of psychology that Maslow hoped would grow out of the Humanistic system: Transpersonal Psychology.

We are used to taking things apart to look at them, to analysing things in order to examine the parts. 'Straight' psychology looks down into the subconscious to find childish, ancestral fears that paralyse and waste energies, but there is another way of looking at things; at the universal perspective of human behaviour. To look at a human being as an organic, whole, functioning unit. To accept that man is a spiritual as well as a psychological being, and to recognise that with the integration of the whole, the sum is greater than its parts. Transpersonal Psychology is a psychology for people living in a world where things happen so fast that questions never get answered. For people who seldom even get the chance to ask the questions because these deal with things of which academic psychology cannot even conceive. At the top of his hierarchy of needs, Maslow said man needs 'Self-Realisation'.

Assagioli likens the psyche to an egg. He suggests in this model that we imagine it divided horizontally into three parts which represent the upper, middle and lower levels of our unconscious minds. The middle part is the area of the present which 'contains' everything that we do not want constantly on our minds, but which can be brought into consciousness from memory.

The lower part is the area of the past, which we can imagine is dark; dark because we do not know what is in it, although it can affect our conscious thinking. It is a changing, structured arrangement of parts which contains all the material, the painful experiences and repressed feelings which cause too much havoc to remain in our memory. This means that in fact we have lost parts of ourselves and if we try to recover these repressed memories and ideas we are set the hard task of coming to terms with the recovered memories and strange tendencies within us. But if they are recovered this should stop many things going on which we cannot control. This lower part holds in fact the greatest seeds to our potential. As well as all the things we push out of memory the 'lower unconscious' also contains things which have never been conscious and are on their way to being conscious. This is because the 'lower unconscious' is in constant contact with the 'collective unconscious', the space around the whole egg, which holds knowledge of everything that humanity has ever known; that is, the 'archetypes' or original patterns or models of our being, which, in the final analysis, we all share.

The upper part, the 'higher unconscious', or supraconscious, is the area of the future, into which we move when we cross the threshold of intuition. It is beyond the everyday awareness and the 'lower unconscious' of the individual and in the future towards which human consciousness seems to be evolving. It is the great womb of potentiality which we all inherit, where human creativity begins to transcend time and space; and which always seems new as a new generation makes contact with it. In the words of the great poets and writers, it is the Divine Imagination.

On the shell of the upper part of the egg, on the border between the 'higher unconscious' and the 'collective unconscious', Assagioli chooses to place what he calls the 'higher self', or the 'transpersonal self'. Again this is only a convenient term for a feature of the unconscious that appears to be the unifying centre of each individual. The 'I' in consciousness (a tiny yolk in the middle of the egg), is only a very small part of our existence. The ego, or personality, is a reflection of that essence, that true Self. We have what can be called a small 'I' and a larger 'I'. The Will is the most direct expression of the Self and the journey of the Will, once it has been set in motion is to try to bring together the apparent polarity between the two and draw this into consciousness. The Will's natural inclination is to transcend the personality limitation through union with something greater or higher.

There are also three corresponding levels of Will. There is the Will of Personal Intention. Then, on another level, there is the Will of the Higher Self, which becomes increasingly conscious the more attuned we are. This is the Will that our Higher Self wishes to incarnate. In Psychosynthesis there are techniques for taking people back to the moment of birth, to reconnect with their choice to be born. Taken back deeply into their essence they contact the impulse to manifest. But there is even another Will; the Universal Will. In religious terms it is the Will of God. The Will of the order of the universe, the unfolding plan, and we can align our Personal and Transpersonal Wills with the unfolding order of the universe.

At some point in the natural development of growth, the Transpersonal Will may exert a 'pull' from above. The pull is felt by the small 'I' as a 'pull' or a 'call'. And this is what is known as a peak experience. There is no language to describe it adequately, except by poetic metaphor, but once the light is shining, you sense the link is made with something much bigger than the personal 'I'. You experience an intelligent energy directed towards an aim, a purpose, which brings an awareness and acceptance of your destiny and a distant sense that somehow you have been given the opportunity to tune into, and participate in, the rhythm of universal life. A feeling that there is a polarity between the human personality as a whole and the Transpersonal Self which can be drawn into a unity. For anyone who knows this, beliefs and cares can never be quite the same again.

The peak experience can also be a more powerful one with an instantaneous sense of unity, as it was for Lynice and Isobel. A sense of 'nothingness', or a oneness with the universe, a direct experience of the ultimate reality and the essential unity of all aspects of reality; a link between the microcosm and the macrocosm, between man and the universe.

This rapid peak experience can sometimes follow the more protracted one. Lorraine experienced both. After her first intuitive realisation when she was looking at Michelangelo's David in Florence, she felt she had emerged from a nightmare. She knew with certainty that her life was again going to change totally. After three weeks in Florence she knew she couldn't sustain the feeling of achievement that the experience had given her, and travelled to Kolmar to see the famous Grunëwalde altar pieces. Immediately she felt an affinity to Grunëwalde in his depiction of the processes of life through Christ. His representation of the absence of light, the darkening of life, his symbol of the agony of having to come through a death. "I felt I had gone through so many deaths, but these deaths had also always contained great hope because I knew it was only like passing through a door. As I walked around to his other paintings they became filled with light and colour and joy and hope, and the whole series became a confirmation of what I had learned in Florence."

By this time her head was brimming with the need to begin something which was already taking on great meaning for her. But in London she found no one to share her thoughts with and this made them instantly impotent. She couldn't think of anything in her own language to put down what she felt. She had seen all this but perhaps, she thought, it wasn't for her. She went into severe depressions for about three weeks. And then she awoke.

"One morning I woke up and the sun was streaming through the window. I hadn't spoken to anyone at all for about three weeks. I walked to the table and thought, this is it, I'm going to have to give up. I was aware of an oak tree growing in a pot on the table, and suddenly I sensed it was alive. I felt, almost felt, the pounding of its energy as a life force. Then my boundaries seemed to leave me. I wasn't aware of me any more. My mind seemed to extend and I became actually part of the process, part of the spirit engaged in this whole, wonderful endeavour called Life. I was aware that that plant was just as important and just as functional as I was. And yet I was unique, but still it was universally a whole thing rolled into one. I felt death didn't matter. Nothing was worth the kind of worry I had been through before. I was at total peace with the world. It was the most extraordinary feeling."

The Self is not the same as the supraconcious and people who have a 'religious' experience or a creative burst from this source are not necessarily linking with Self. Whichever way it happens, a peak experience which does link with Self, gives a glimpse in consciousness that there is a whole around which the parts must be co-ordinated to create harmony and balance, and your own personal link with it. The key to self-realisation or 'individuation' as Jung calls it, is balance. Every function of life is a polarity; as the sun is to the moon, the dark to the light, the conscious to the unconscious. The process of growth is towards balance in every area of our psyche; to avoid identifying with either of two opposite poles. It is the balancing of opposites. It is to understand the value of the mind as well as the heart; of a reason as well as of feeling; of sensitivity or receptivity as well as activity; of masculine as well as feminine – the potential for which we all have in our being.

This 'balanced adjustment and creative synthesis' can be

reached by some in a fairly harmonious way by means of a gradual decrease in the swing of the pendulum which swings between two extremes. But for most of us it is a long, painful process. Once the Will to Grow has been set in motion, the psyche is beginning its battle towards balance. In a natural progression, the peak experience that triggers the conscious link with Self will come at a point where a certain amount of balance has been achieved in the psychological body, in the personal 'I' or personality. Self-actualisation can, in some cases, correspond to the movement towards personal synthesis, and after the link with Self, the process does not stop, it simply becomes more conscious. The process of balancing continues at different levels of the personal and transpersonal and in various proportions because there is a natural tendency towards development and harmony in all human functions on all levels.

The transpersonal Self shines down while the personal Self shines up. It is a dual process and therefore it is possible for the link, the thread between the two, to be triggered at virtually any stage, not necessarily in the nature sequence of balancing. Liz feels that because of her extreme *im*balance, the Self was forced almost in desperation to throw out a light for her to catch a glimpse. If her psyche had continued to go on the way it had been, it would have collapsed totally. The Self had to offer some kind of new experience, of change and breakthrough in order to shift around all the bits and pieces and to force them to begin to come back together again. It is a question of extremes. Either you get the link in a natural way because of the balance. Or, because of the opposite extreme of total imbalance, the link is produced in an unnatural way.

There is another unnatural way in which the link can occur. It is a potentially dangerous way and one which should therefore be mentioned. For Lynice the trigger was a drug. "When I took the LSD I saw behind the outer realities we see around us. It was as though a veil had been covering something much better and I saw behind that veil. I could see people clearly too. It was as though they had been wearing masks and I could suddenly see what they were really thinking and feeling deep inside. For me it was a very positive experience and it meant a strong outpouring of love for other people and a wish to help them, because when I saw behind the mask I saw a lot of pain. There was also a point at which I felt I was going to understand something about myself but this would not quite come to me. It was as though I had something on the tip of my tongue but I couldn't get hold of it."

The important point is that she experienced this knowledge without working for it; without any effort on her part. She jumped the gun and then had to work for several years to bring it into her consciousness. A drug *can* be a trigger but it is also a tremendous risk. If you go straight into the experience of the collective unconscious without proper preparation, there is the danger that you will be unable to cope with it. Because you do not know how the drug got you to that place, you cannot know the road. To reconnect with this spiritual experience you then depend on the drug. But, more important, this is an artificial glimpse. When you use a drug you see the light at the end of the tunnel, but when you travel through experience you can know that it is the tunnel that has value, not its end.

For three years after she took the drug, Lynice sank into incredible depressions and felt ill most of the time. It took her a long while to realise what was actually happening. Slowly it became clear that the LSD had done something physically to her. It had loosened her from her physical body and un-knowingly she was having some psychic experiences. But because she wasn't functioning properly within her body, she was pulled away by her emotions. It was not until several years later, when she met a priest of the Christian Community, a new form of religion based on Rudolf Steiner's work, that she could pour out her soul. She explained to him that she felt there were strange forces at work which she couldn't understand, and that there was something oppressing her that she couldn't put her finger on. He made her see things about herself which helped her to understand her life and her destiny. He made her realise that during this crisis time she was having to come to terms with an awareness that had happened through the LSD. People who have not developed to a certain level of spirituality cannot cope with these experiences. You can only begin to understand the underlying realities of the world as you develop within yourself. He helped her to realise that she had much work to do to catch up with herself and to cope with life again on her own. Paradoxically of course, she knows that all this pain was right for her. Through this she could come to an understanding of her future work. But it is a heavy price to pay.

The West today has become totally materialistic. Our incessant drive for personal ego power is disrupting the earth, the only piece of the universe we possess and are wholly responsible for. Technological power is used to enslave us. We go to the moon but we are not conscious of our true selves. Each of us is under the illusion of separateness, we think we are alone and cut off, yet increasingly we hope that there must be something more. It is as though we have pushed self-actualisation to the point of boredom and dissatisfaction with the way things are. The sense of the 'I', the gratifying ego, is not so grand after all. In this intensely materialistic age we have become lopsided and unbalanced; we have completely lost contact with the spiritual world and with the realisation that man is a spiritual being in a universe which is spiritual in nature.

Human beings, says Laurens Van der Post, can endure everything except meaninglessness and that is the plague from which we suffer at the moment. He says that to go to new geographical places has helped him to go to new places within himself. Exploring helped him find an area in his own spirit, and therefore in the human spirit in general, where enormous transforming energies are available. These energies restore one's original longing to do things, and because they suggest something more than the everyday life around us, they set up a longing to become part of the immense process we get glimpses of in nature.

A few people have begun to realise the importance of being part of a universe and the importance of finding the right path to who they really are; the need to narrow the gap between internal and external power. In becoming who we are, by taking responsibility for ourselves into our own hands, we affect the lives of everyone else around us. The hopes of the few can become the hopes of the many. And think of the potential if this mass longing should mushroom into mass Willing. Humanity is ready to set its Will into motion towards full global self-realisation.

A Path with Heart

*"But how will I know for sure
whether a path has heart or not?"*
*"Anybody would know that. The
trouble is nobody asks the
question."*

Carlos Castaneda in *The Teachings of Don Juan*

The energy gathered round that linking with the Transpersonal Self is phenomenal, quite unearthly. It is like a surge from somewhere 'out there' shrieking at you. 'You can be bigger too.' It is an energy of tremendous optimism, in a personal sense but also with a wider meaning. A certainty that, in spite of all the tragic difficulties and confrontations, the world will be all right.

The effect is shattering.

The linking of the Personal 'I' and the inner Self breaks down inner references, and the personal identity is shaken. It is a deep inner, and completely alien, experience which can be totally traumatic. Through their early years most people gather around them some sense of personality, a hardening at the surface to protect themselves. No one could survive on their original sensitive level without doing so. But once this crisis of growth is triggered, either from the outside or the inside, it guarantees to break through the hardening and the world suddenly falls down. Like the emergence of a butterfly from the cocoon, the inner being grows too big to be held and must burst through. We are breaking, like a rocket, through to a new stage and every aspect of life seems different. The old has little relevance to the new. Relationships are inadequate, work takes on a different meaning and the rules of behaviour laid down by society seem off-key. You are forced to take a conscious look at the meaning of your life and see where on earth you are going.

For almost everyone who undergoes this, it is a period of acute loneliness unless there is someone else near who has had a similar experience. There are no adequate words to describe the state, communication must come through some kind of shared inner feeling rather than through the words transmitted. And, once you have accepted that this is the path to your destiny, and realise the inevitability of the upheaval it must bring, you know you'll need courage. The rhythm of your new life will be completely out of step with the old one. Balanced to a certain extent in the Personal 'I' or personality, you must begin a further kind of balancing in the Transpersonal 'I', and endeavour to harmonise them. All the rules change and life becomes a constant paradox.

It is painful. It is exciting. It is inevitable. The tragedy for some people is that during the long process of this peak experience, they are treated as though they are breaking down, when in reality they are breaking up to break through.

So there is an 'I' that knows me. A part of me that knows who I really am and what I really want to do and what I need to be able to do it. A part that knows that the code of society had tied me up in knots, but that tells me I can now, still within that system, really be me. That there is a real me to be. I know that I know something, but what do I know? Now that I know that I know I have somewhere to go and something to do, how do I know what that is? How do I know what I must do? How do I know that this really is me? What chaos! This energy tells me there is something going on, an evolutionary process and that the boundaries of my life aren't fixed. There are so many more things to know and understand, the horizon is endless. The pilot light is lit and I have accepted my destiny. I have accepted that if I want to make this journey, upheaval is inevitable. But if I give up all the security of the way that I know, how do I know I won't sink into obscurity? I have fought and gathered my defences to survive this far, and now I leap into the dark. How crazy. How do I know that this is the right path? How do I *know* to trust this intuition?

There is only one answer. And that is, leave it to chance.

When you look back over your life and see what an extraordinary and fundamental part coincidence or chance, in the form of lucky breaks, has played, you might wonder how you ever made it here. But during the peak experience, when it looks almost as though the Self is taking over, life begins to offer such positive, pertinent, almost outrageous coincidences that you are forced to sit up and take notice. It feels as though something outside you is taking you on, determined to see you through this phase. At the beginning there is such a strong sense of 'protection', you feel that everything has been taken out of your hands. In the terms of Psychosynthesis, the 'Higher Self' is energising particular parts of your personality in order to make you go in a certain direction. And at this point you are conscious of it. This protection seems determined to hold you up for however long it takes you to reach the point where you totally trust your own intuition and the rightness of your path. When everything around you seems impossibly chaotic and unworkable, the Self lets you know you aren't alone. It keeps you going by dangling carrots of coincidence, or synchronicities.

Synchronicity, as Jung explains it, is 'meaningful coincidence', the 'science' that Chinese theories of medicine and philosophy are based on. This is how the Chinese Book of Changes, the *I Ching*, works and how tarot cards turn out to be so significant at exactly the moment you need them. This is the same underlying principle in astrology and in the old way of consulting Oracles. The classical Chinese texts did not ask what causes what, but rather, what 'likes' to occur with what. The idea is that inner and outer events which are not caused one by the other, 'like' to cluster together at certain times. Synchronistic events, says Jung, almost always accompany the crucial phases in the process of individuation. But usually they pass unnoticed, because people haven't learned to watch out for such coincidences and make them meaningful.

At this stage the Self virtually hurls them down like thunderbolts to make known its intentions and to indicate the direction in which your life-stream is moving. It is up to us to grab these fragments of chance. The carrots present themselves in remarkable guises. During the inner struggle you are given exactly what you need to get through. Out on a limb and afraid you cannot cope, something will turn up which confirms you are on the right track. The means are given to ensure that you will succeed. If, for instance, your deep knowing says you must give up your work for a short time in order to wander, for some meaningful but as yet unspecific reason, by some mysterious chance the financial means might be given for you to do this. Suddenly you are a magnet for what you need; money from a forgotten job, a windfall, a tax refund. Quite innocent in themselves, but they make a pattern for you which is devastating in its confirmation that you are doing the right thing.

When Lorraine returned from Florence she ran around to friends in a state of panic wondering what she was going to do with her great vision. To be able to create, she felt she had to have something concrete to rely on and applied for a teachers' course. She was frightened and insecure about the future, but at the same time she knew she needed to concentrate her mind on the paintings. It was at this point she met someone who had seen her work and believed in it, and he agreed to finance her minimally for a year. This was sufficient to prove whether or not she could do it.

When Lynice was still with her community in Corsica, she heard about Emerson College, the adult centre for training and research based on Anthroposophy, the work of Rudolf Steiner. She knew with certainty she must go there, but she owned a herd of goats with no one else to look after them, and in any case had no money for the return fare to England. Yet within weeks a friend arrived in Corsica who knew about goats and was longing to look after some and another friend gave her some money. She saw the College and knew it right, but still she couldn't afford to study there. Instead she

decided to take a job as housemother for maladjusted
children at one of the Steiner schools in Gloucester and after
a year she applied for a county grant. "When I got one I knew
it was a gift from somewhere else," she says. She had 'by
chance' taken a job in the only county in England which gave
grants for colleges outside the state system and to people who
had only lived in the area for a short time.

Liz, on the other hand, was not given material means.
When she looks back, though, she realises she didn't need
this, so the intuition didn't bother to produce it. "But it did
give me the most remarkable knack of being in the right place
at the right time. I would suddenly drop everything and rush
to England and find I had arrived on the one evening that
someone who proved important happened to be passing
through. Or I would be in a bookshop where exactly the right
book would catch my eye and I would have exactly enough
money in my purse. It has produced many things."

Because her peak experience came so early, at the age of
nineteen, and at a time when her emotional life was seriously
disturbed, Liz knew she would need to do a lot of work in
understanding herself as a woman before she could make a
living experience of it. Although for many years afterwards
her life was in constant contradiction, she did have an
immediate sense of trust in her knowing, in her intuition,
from the moment of the peak experience. In fact, as early as
six or seven she had experienced some 'funny flashes', a sense
that 'something' was dragging her through life. "It must have
been something I have always known in a sense, because after
the peak experience I plunged into things, taking them
completely on trust. When I suddenly realised the meaning in
this experience of there being something other than a
personal ego in me, I behaved ridiculously."

After the peak experience she spent the summer in New
York. Without any hesitation she went wandering around the
streets of New York at 3 a.m., managing narrowly to avoid
situations in which she should have been raped or robbed. "I
was still glowing inside with the magic of this thing and I felt
it had an effect on other people. I ended up being friends with
people who would otherwise have robbed me." Or she would

fly back to California with literally 10c in her pocket and hope that the person she rang there would know something for her to do. Even though she was negative in herself at that time, this sense was so positive and strong that she went blindly into things and the 'knowing' brought her through it emotionally.

Yet there was a time when the certainty died. Married and divorced while still at college, she went through acute depression when she left to start work, and everything seemed to collapse. At the age of twenty-four, four or five years after the experience, she completely lost faith. "That is why I think I went into a second marriage," she says. "I suddenly panicked and when I looked back I began to think I had been crazy."

She blanked out the whole experience by trying to go back to a normal life, and living in the way most people do. She gave up astrology to be at home and cook dinner like a model wife. But after six months she felt so claustrophobic, she couldn't stand it. She had lowered her consciousness and was suffocating. She couldn't live like that and knew she had to go back to the way she had been before. "I wasn't sure if it was still there, but I found it so patently was. It was like a joke, the synchronicities that happened to confirm it for me. Including getting a job in the music business so I could come to England to work in astrology again. It made me laugh for a long time, but from then on I didn't worry about it again."

For some people the carrots must of necessity be dramatic to make their point. For others such as Isobel, who seems always to have had this sense of rightness and of being on her path, who has come through on a more gentle oscillation of the pendulum, the lessons need be taught in little more than a whisper. For her it has seemed at times rather more a question of sitting on the path and playing it out in front of her. Having initiated the process, it could be left to itself. As a nurse she was already training her intuition. In New Zealand where nurses were not always trained for every actuality, she was forced to take responsibility for herself. She trusted her perception and she always found it easy to accept startling synchronicities. Once you are on the path this is the natural way for things to be and it has never surprised her when things 'just turn up'. Since she first came to England and needed a flat, the right opportunity has always presented itself. It was always the most natural thing in the world to 'put in her wish' and wait for it to turn up. "It didn't occur to me to doubt it," she says. "I would decide to do something and do it. If something crossed my path I thought 'oh well, I'll do it'. My life knew what it wanted and intuition fell into place for me."

For most of us, the lesson is more difficult to learn. There are moments during the confusing months following the peak experience when nothing seems to fit and caught in a limbo between two kinds of understanding, two qualitatively different worlds, life looks grim. Looking back at that original energy of purpose, you hang on to the certainty that it must be real. But something else has to keep you going. When things became so bad for Lynice that she couldn't take another step, something always turned up to tell her she was right. Someone or something significant had to appear. A sense of her own inner growth also proved a confirmation. Each time she survived a crisis, she knew she had come out of it a very different person. Dreams, too, were quite clearly a help. Not the ordinary ones we all have, but especially powerful ones which had important spiritual significance. Pictures which she had to interpret for herself, but ones which in fact she tried not to tamper with too much. Such dreams are so highly symbolic that it is better to leave them in pictures and to interpret them inwardly rather than intellectually. These were an expression, a confirmation, that she was going through something extraordinary of which she wasn't consciously aware, but that she was being guided.

Lorraine found her own kind of confirmation. Any painter who has a message, she says, knows that the first time he shows his work, other people will connect to it or not through pure gut reaction. She was scared at her first exhibition but, strangely, the three paintings which she herself held in doubt, were the only ones criticised. This experience proved to her how people instinctively do know about good work and she knew then that she could trust her own work in terms of public reaction. "This was my first major step towards confidence."

When Diana made up her mind to return to Esalen full-time at twenty-five, to continue to work on herself, she literally set herself down on the doorstep and told them she wanted a job. She couldn't afford to pay for the workshops, but the system is such that if you work on staff, the workshops are given free. The jobs are all manual and as a staff member you begin by working for nothing except meals and find your own place to stay. Of course everyone on earth seemed to want to live there and it was virtually impossible to get a job. She stayed around for two and a half months which took great will. Her father sent her a little money to sustain her during that time and occasionally she got a day's work. But finally the manager told her she must leave.

At this point Diana met Selig Morganrath. He is the man mainly responsible for the spectacular architecture of the grounds at Esalen, in which every building blends in with the environment, and nothing stands out as being man-made. Morganrath, like a 'sixty-eight year old elf with long white hair', worked magic with plants. He organically grew all the food for Esalen and was convinced that if only people would go back to nature, they would have no problems. For some inexplicable reason he said Diana could work in the gardens for nothing. She had never gardened before and could do nothing very special. She did the weeding and digging and helped with anything she couldn't ruin. Morganrath was impressed. No one else cared much about working and she really had worked hard. After a week he and his wife Barbara put her on staff.

There was absolutely no doubt about it, she was in the right place. They were her teachers and she learned so much from them about life and nature. It was very different from just being around nature. By caring for plants, she learned to care for life. Putting her hands in the earth and working with the earth was symbolic of life. Nature was co-operating and nurturing life rather than using and destroying it. By gardening she became one with nature. What emerged was an incredible facility with nature which she simply hadn't known about. She didn't know anything about gardening, but in her mind she would ask the plants. "If I had to prune a tree I said 'okay, if I don't know how to do it you'll have to help me'. I would talk to them and they would symbolically talk to me. I could make every plant healthy and people would bring me their sick plants. I learned that plants were not just things, but have essence as well. I feel I discovered for myself the subtle energies in plants." Something special was happening. Selig and Barbara would tell her the elemental rules, but she felt the plants themselves taught her through her intuition. She became consciously aware of some kind of spiritual relationship with nature, and whenever she began to doubt her path, this would always come back to her to confirm it.

After a time, the carrots stop dangling in such an outrageous way. From that point on, it is a much more subtle process. To begin with there is a lot of rubbish to clear in the search for trust in your intuition. Once you are no longer using a shovel, it can become more subtle and refined. Affirmation can come in more gentle ways. "I can sniff when it is beginning to come," says Liz. "I came to England on its directive, I just knew I had to come here and everything would begin to unfold, although I didn't have a clear-cut idea. Everything I have done has had that patina on it and I've followed it implicitly. The time to begin something and the time to end it. It lets me know the end of cycles. Something will appear if I start waking up and, if I don't start waking up, then I get kicked from behind."

No violent voice, no great revelations, just a feeling of certainty. Of course it is easy to be thrown from this sense, to feel doubt and panic, but gradually you learn that it is the times when you don't obey your intuition, that you fall down hardest. It is often the easier way, but you will pay three times over. Somehow you know that the rightness is still there. Not trusting your intuition is not trusting yourself. The more you like yourself, the more you trust that. And at the end of the 'test' you realise that however hard the path, it somehow has to be right. The link with Self and ultimately with God and the universe is real. The path has its hills, but everything you need to stay on that path, will appear.

Knowing is perceiving Rightness. Knowing is trusting your intuition.

2

Notes towards
a Supreme Fiction

"In the uncertain light of single, certain truth,
Equal in living changingness to the light
In which I meet you, in which we sit at rest,
For a moment in the central of our being,
The vivid transparence that you bring is peace.'

From the *Selected Poems* of Wallace Stevens

It must be Abstract

*"You must become an ignorant man again
And see the sun again with an ignorant eye
And see it clearly in the idea of it."*

Wallace Stevens *Notes Towards A Supreme Fiction*

Truth, says American poet Wallace Stevens, must come abstracted from any kind of conventional experience. We each individually have our own certain truth which we have to find; a truth which speaks to us without our having to put it into logical language. From the moment we are born, we are influenced by the people around us to look at the world in which we live in a particular kind of way. We give things names, like horse or chair or Susan, and because we have a name we think we really understand it. We are given a generalised description of things that everyone agrees with. That description depends on the descriptive words used and what is attached to those particular words.

Says the Yaqui man of knowledge Don Juan to Carlos Castaneda in *Teachings of Don Juan*, there is too much use of words in talking and writing. Words always force us to feel enlightened and when we turn to face the world they fool us. Words are illusory, they deceive. Having a word is no way of understanding it. Words are only a momentary description, but once you have written something down, it is difficult to start again, because then you feel caught by it. In *Tales of*

Power, Don Juan explains how in American Indian mythology everything is either Tonal or Nagual. Tonal is that in our universe which we can name, but beyond that is Nagual – that which can never be named but can only be experienced. Tonal begins at birth and ends with death and the disintegration of the ego. Nagual never ends, it is the spiritual within the body. Michael Polanyi talked too about tacit and explicit knowledge. Explicit knowledge is formulated in words and maps and mathmatical symbols. Tacit knowledge is the knowledge of what we are in the process of doing before we express it in words and symbols. On a walk in the country, we can absorb a knowledge of the scenery around us and appreciate its beauty without necessarily describing it to ourselves in words. Behind the barrier of language we can understand ideas which are limited once they are put into words.

Of course we need words, but the power to describe things in rational terms, which should be a helpful guardian to us, becomes instead a despotic guard who tells us that this is all there is. We must learn to read between the lines, to see the coloured thread which makes the brightly coloured patterns through the warp and weft. Standing in a room our ordinary 'rings of power' are making the room. But with another kind of 'ring of power' we can spin a different room in a different world. With this other ring of power, the power of pure individual imagination, it is possible to break up the commonplace description of things and find another one.

Today, for example, art students don't look at a chair and think of a chair, but are encouraged to try and loosen the usual description they have been given and have lived with for so long. They are persuaded to look at lines and shadows and shapes and the relationship between the chair and other things. In this way they can begin to see something quite different. By focusing attention on things we don't normally notice, or pay attention to – like the lights on a tree and the shadows on the leaves – the more feasible it becomes that there is another way of experiencing this world, and the more we can understand that there might be other ways of seeing.

Another way of experiencing ourselves than that which is wished upon us.

We each have a rational description of ourselves created by those around us. To see ourselves in a different way means we must be prepared to lose our personal history. By becoming too much attached to the personal image of ourselves given to us as we grow up, we are forced to act in a certain way because people expect it from us. We behave for a social purpose. Don Juan tells Carlos that in order to become a man of knowledge, he must loosen the mask. In other words he must lose the idea that other people have about him, upon which stage he acts. He must lose his self-importance.

From the moment we can talk, we do what everyone else does by imitating our parents and our society. And in the West in particular, we are influenced by our education to think in a rational, intellectual way. Reason has to give a description in order to make a distinction, but when this process is carried to excess, we forget that we also have the power to experience ourselves in a different way. Reason makes us forget that we are only a description, and traps us in a vicious circle through which we never emerge in our lifetimes. The description we have of ourselves and our world is only one part of reality. We must discover the rest and use this totality.

There are times when we must shut off and get away from the descriptions we are putting on things and become 'an ignorant man again'. We must take what we look at, all our traditional experience and strip it of its intellectualised meaning to make it our own experience. Like the trees in winter, we should bare it to its outline, to become aware that as well as objects, we are also perceivers, and to realise that we have a non-explicit centre within us which is our link with man's potential and the source of our movement towards what Stevens calls 'the creative imagination'. Or in William Blake's terms, 'the divine imagination'. We are capable of being in mysteries, united with phenomena, become them momentarily without the need to reach out for fact and reason.

The work of the imagination is concerned with the one, while reason deals with the many. Science, unlike religion and art asks 'what happens?', never who does it?' So science continues to make us more and more estranged from our individuality. Scientific experiment in its quantative manner forgets the one unobserved element, the observer. It is never thought relevant to ask *who* is working at the atomic research station. This is not considered to be relevant. Yet in no circumstances are we ever objective, because each one of us selects. The candle of imagination lights our world, not the dead formulae that have for a long time made us see in clichés. For a thought to have relevance we must feel it, we must soak ourselves in its idea. It is the sense or intuition of an idea that makes it mean something. If you don't feel for it, you are not going to bother with it. Like when learning a language, things suddenly begin to light up. Reality catches your eye and winks at you. Or like in choosing a poem (which is closer to music than the rational prose statement) you pick the one which hits you to begin with, the one that speaks to you without need to put it into logical language, the one that makes you feel the invisible reality beyond the external. For there you find the space in between to think and feel from your own experience.

There is another language to be learned before we can enter the world all over again. There is a world within a world, and imagination is the connection between the two. We cannot ignore the outer or the inner, but we in the West have veered too far into the world of reason. We must view the world as more than its material reality. We suffer through our sense of loss of a central creed and the need to know what is behind reality. We have to break out of the shackles of materialism and intellectualism which persuade us to believe that the universe is a great mechanism and that man is an accident in nature and different from her; that man is a being *in* this world, not *of* it. We need to regain a picture of the oneness of all life and the knowledge that everything and everyone belongs to the beginning, and derives from a vast continuum of creative thought, a creative intelligence. We must again see man as a being of spirit, which is a concept lost for thousands of years. We are all energetic and resourceful personalities that have been persuaded towards wealth and power and pleasure. We have not realised that the purely personal locks off other kinds of energies and cuts off circulation. If man goes on thinking he is living in a dead universe, we shall always have planetary problems. If we bring in this other factor, there is nothing that cannot be done to redeem our planet.

Seeing everything as a whole, we might then begin to raise the possibility that we all exist as fully developed entities before we are born and that we cannot die. If we could grasp this idea, the anxiety about death would disappear. We would see that a spiritual entity has its own evolution, and that the only responsibility it has in that evolution is to itself. For Lynice, Liz, Isobel and Diana, there is no question that they have lived before and come back many times in the process of training to become totally free beings who can connect with God. They see earth as a training ground for the spirit of man.

The implication of this idea is that we choose our destiny. We have each chosen to reincarnate through the parents we are born to and are prepared to live the life we have chosen, however that is to be. In a sense we come down to rediscover what we already know (taken to its limit we can see that we all know everything). On this particular great new adventure we are searching for the wisdom to learn what we already know. This is something that Liz senses strongly. When she first studied astrology, it was familiar to her. She remembers thinking she knew all this, she had been here before. "It was like asking how I could have forgotten this, I've known it all my life." She had an immediate understanding of what it was about, and it never gave her a problem. Of course her knowledge then was nothing compared to what it is now, and she expects to be learning all her life.

The peak experience emphasises this. It seems merely to confirm something that at the back of your being you have known all along. It confirms a sense of rightness that you could never have put into words, and enables you to go forward along that path.

Every child, says Jean Liedloff in *The Continuum Concept,* is born with the sense of rightness within him. At birth, he has seeds of the unfettered knowledge of the Continuum, drawn from all the collective positive experience that humanity has ever had. He is therefore born with certain expectations, the same expectations that every child for thousands of years has had in order to begin the process of maturing into an adult. He expects a minimum number of consecutive experiences and if these are not met, then the following experiences – as important as they may be – will not contribute properly to the maturing of the adult.

A child in a primitive society still does have those expectations met. He is continuously held from the moment he is born. As a baby he is carried across his mother's back and given the opportunity to see a wide variety of scenes. But we in the West who have changed the system comparatively recently, thwart these expectations from the moment the child is born. From birth he meets the wrong sort of experience. He is left in his cot for long periods of time and has far less contact with his mother than a primitive child has. Carried around in a pram, he lacks stimulation because he is given no width of vision. This instantly sets up longing and neglectedness as a fundamental way of life. "For the child 'self' is wanting and waiting. 'Other' is withholding and unresponsive." These conditions may go unnoticed simply because we don't know any other way of life.

As a child, the primitive person is treated as a small adult and given every opportunity to develop as such. He does not demand his mother's full attention, nor does he receive it. He is too much involved in living in the here and now. He is allowed to use his own sense of danger and will avoid it instinctively. In the West we are constantly held back from danger and saved from pain. If a mother is anxious that her child should not fall off the chair, the child will tend to oblige, and fall. Its social impulse is to fulfill expectations even if it goes against self-preservation. Our instincts are cut off. The native child is allowed in on everything that the parents say and do. He is left to understand what he can. Everything he does is of great interest to the parents but there is no question of imposing influence, least of all to coerce by threat or punishment. We, on the other hand, are forced to understand things by our system of education and immediately we are faced with the conflict between what we can comprehend and what is expected of us.

From the moment we are born, we increasingly lose our sense of rightness, of the continuum which "can build a freedom from the fringe liabilities of the intellect". Intellect is the great barrier in our society. Reason spends its whole time splitting things up. It cannot think of wholeness. Of course we need the reasoning mind, but we also need to go deeper. Since there are no assured systems of belief, all we can hope for is a conscious link with the basic questions, to which we hope there will never be answers. We are approaching myth sideways.

Myth is that which goes beneath the surface of things, to images beyond the individual person and situation. We have a story beneath our lives that has universal significance. The stories have arisen out of people's questions. There is no way to express the meaning of myth, but it is important to ask the questions. This is enough to open a channel and provide a new life. We are seeking in modern terms, by mythological methods, the mysteries of thresholds, of death and rebirth, of pattern and unity. We are engaged in a search, a quest on two levels. Man in search of himself is on an inward as well as outward journey. It is a personal experience to the point where personal experience ceases to be personal and becomes a mythological archetypal experience. It is a journey of ego to find a greater self. We are heroes in the face of a challenge to find reconciliation, in the poet W.B. Yeats' terms, between the passionate and the celestial bodies.

Don Juan tells Carlos that there is only one real world but there is another way of experiencing it. There is a separate reality that is equally real. Not an external world out there, but a world inside in which you experience things in a different way, which you pictorially create by spinning it. The world is objective and subjective too. There are many things which prevent us from experiencing the world in this second way. To begin there is fear of the unknown. We cling to the usual and habitual. Then there is the make-believe power of false intellectual courage. For a new idea to come through, the mind must be foggy, so the depths can take over. With a falsely strong framework, nothing can come through. All the most inspired theories of rational men have come in intuitive flashes. But as Don Juan suggests, the greatest difficulty lies in recognising their rightness; in trimming the spirit impeccably; in listening inwardly to know the moment when to do this or that. Rightness presents possibilities which we do or don't take. There is a right time and place in which decisions can be made to approach that "twilight crack between two worlds", the magic time in myth of dawn or dusk. The meeting edge between light and dark.

Rudolf Steiner was born with the facility for 'seeing' the spiritual reality as well as the material. From the beginning it caused problems in his life simply because he did not realise that no one else saw things in the way he did. It was obvious from the time he started school that he had a very powerful mind. He trained as a scientist, but later worked in everything from geology, physics and mathematics, to poetry and philosophy. Yet he continually had great difficulty in communicating his other, 'seeing' sense.

He experienced spiritual evolution in terms of a series of 'thresholds' beyond the physical world, which could be crossed only after intense preparation. Immediately you leave the physical plane and cross the first threshold from our 'mineral' world in which everything is firmly established in space, you enter the 'plant' world, the etheric or elementary world, in which nothing has form. Like Alice awakening into the bewildering new world of Wonderland, nothing is recognisable as it is in the normal world; nothing is static within boundaries. To cross each threshold we must grow from within and no one should attempt even the lowest realm of the 'supersensible' without careful strengthening within themselves.

It was through the use of mescaline and other hallucinogenic drugs that Don Juan helped to loosen the foundations of his disciple Castaneda's rational mind; to break up the perceptions and move him towards a sense of the irrational. Drugs, as some people have discovered, can bring insights and illuminations but also illusions, and, as we have seen, they can be dangerous. Nor, as Don Juan admits at the end, are they necessary. He used them merely as a way of testing Castaneda's seriousness of purpose. There are an increasing number of 'transcenders' who try to climb this particular spiritual path and who have great facility in moving into inner space. But there they can come unstuck. As Diana warns, "Until I discovered Psychosynthesis, I was an unclear being walking around with a large number of disjointed esoteric and spiritual concepts, none of which made sense or fitted into any coherent pattern. I was truly confused and filled with lack of understanding."

To transcend has little value in our lives if we cannot function properly down here on earth. When Liz had her peak experience at nineteen, her emotions were in tatters. Her 'knowing' told her that she must consciously integrate these before she could use her knowing as a living experience. After trying 'straight' psychology which didn't work, she tried everything to get help with her emotional life. She learned about spiritual healing, about the occult, and how to develop astral vision. But none of this helped because she didn't know what was wrong. She soon realised that spiritual knowledge cannot help on the personality level. Until the personality, the vehicle we use on earth, is firmly integrated in the body, the spiritual has no value in itself at all.

If people 'live in the sky' and find they cannot get back down to earth, they are lost in this world, which is a terrifying and quite frequent experience. There is too much questionable material which has led people astray. Nor do they realise that psychic is not necessarily spiritual. Some people tend to get caught up in the phenomena when the relevance is what is behind it all. More often than not, psychics and clairvoyants are not highly spiritually involved. Perception of the spiritual kind is meaningful and constructive, not just new and out of the ordinary like the phenomena which science is beginning to investigate. What causes the phenomena might be spiritual, but there is a qualitative difference. There is a remarkable source behind it.

Steiner, too, was adamant in saying that the way for us to achieve spirituality at this stage in our evolution is by working in the world, not leaving it to find spiritual enlightenment. We cannot work only by ourselves, but must bring these qualities into our relationships with other people. After twenty years of intense inner study, he presented Anthroposophy, a science of the spirit. He gave an outline for many new paths, in education, in medicine, in agriculture, in painting and sculpture and in the use of colour. He also presented a new form of dance called Eurythmy. This can be used purely as an art form but also in a healing sense, and it is in this way that Eurythmy helped Lynice greatly when she was at her lowest ebb.

Each time you speak a sound, the larynx creates a form. This form goes through the whole physical body and expresses an inner feeling. If you say the sound 'Ah' (as in father), this has a feeling of wonder of opening yourself out, like standing in front of the sun. In Eurythmy, the form of speech sounds is made visible through gesture. Steiner gave indications for gestures for the movement in space which lies behind things like speech, colours and 'soul moods' such as sympathy and antipathy, fear and hate. In music the gestures arise from the tones and intervals and the moods of major and minor. If a poem is spoken the eurythmist makes the appropriate gestures with the whole of his body although the arm gestures are particularly visible. He moves in space in geometric forms and the movement of space around him must be made particularly conscious.

Whereas modern dance is arbitrary and created according to the moods of the choreographer, Eurythmy is something precise. A person capable of 'seeing' would see these forms and would be aware that they were working with 'etheric forces'. Originally Steiner presented it with special costumes and veils of different colours. The costume colour expressed the movement and the veil colour expressed the feeling. The veils helped the audience to be aware of the movement of air in each gesture.

In his concern that we should work within the world, he also pointed out that in most meditations, which follow the Eastern pattern, you are asked to withdraw from the senses and try to reach inner space by being shut off from outer stimulation. He felt that the Eastern way, though right for its time and its people, was not right for our stage of Western evolution. We have made a progression and cannot go back. He, in fact, gave an opposite path to meditation, that of very exact observation. Few of us, he said, observe the things around us precisely. We see in a vague hazy way, but should observe the leaves of plants for example and watch how they grow. We should notice the shapes of people's noses and what they are wearing. As Lynice says, "Steiner also showed how one can develop and activate one's thinking. Our thoughts are but pale reflections of a spiritual reality. They are passive. If we can learn to penetrate and control our thought process without allowing our thoughts to control us by buzzing incessantly in our heads, then we can reach the spirit through active thinking."

As Wallace Stevens says in his poems, if we work from the fact that plants and metals and stones and just about everything else has a reality behind it that we don't fully see, we can establish a celebration of the natural world and what it can do for the imagination. Keeping conscious observation is a way of bringing the Will into perception.

This kind of observation came easily to Diana, who has always had a very close relationship to nature. Through much lone contact through long walks, hiking, climbing and camping, she has spent a large part of her life communing with nature. Whenever she was down, she would go to the woods to find peace again. "I never knew consciously what I was doing, but somehow I possessed some kind of 'knowing' that this is what my organism needed in order to heal itself. I was at one point quite dependent on nature for serenity and awareness of my sense of being. Nature became early my religious experience as well as my psychological therapist. In times of severe unhappiness I would go alone to nature and scream, cry, yell, pray, write reams of poetry; doing whatever felt right."

The Wise Virgin

We have no solidity, we are boundless. We only have the solidity we see to make our passage on earth convenient. Our first responsibility is to our own inner space and our own intelligence. It is this we must work on. Each of us is given a musical note of our own to contribute to the universal symphony. We must learn to play it properly.

It must change

"Two things of opposite natures seem to depend
On one another, as a man depends
On a woman, day on night, the imagined
On the real. This is the origin of change."

Wallace Stevens *Notes Towards A Supreme Fiction*

There are no certain truths, said poet Wallace Stevens. Since
we live perpetually within the question we cannot have a
creed. Nothing can be ordained, there is no place at which we
can arrive and say, 'I believe this and all will be secure.' As
food transforms our bodies, so experiences are transformed by
what each of us does. We all have to learn through our own
experience. Truth is living and so, like the patterns of the sky
reflected in a lake, it must constantly change. And we too
must feel a constant freshness in ourselves. We need to
"gather strength against a system which would freeze our
humanity, which would push us into being automatons and
into a way of thinking that makes us believe we are cogs in a
machine."

Jean Liedloff suggests that particularly in the civilised
West, we are deprived from birth of our deep inner sense of
the continuum of life. If we are dispossessed of our sense of
rightness at such an early age, it seems inevitable that we
should begin life with a nagging longing for security from
outside; a need for security which the methods of education
adopted by our society perpetuate. We are forced, by

example and training, into a search for an elusive sense of security in something outside ourselves – we find something to depend on in relationships, in work, in wealth and position, in status. And this yearning for security coerces us into assuming roles and adopting habits which will reinforce our illusion. Habits, says Arthur Koestler are the core of stability and ordered behaviour. They also have a tendency to become mechanised and to reduce man to the state of a conditioned automaton. The creative act is an act of liberation – the defeat of habit by originality.

Habit is hard to break; we hold on so fast to our memories and stability. But during a peak experience you are forced to let go. Once you have chosen the inevitable period of limbo on that 'spiritual' path, insecurity becomes the only certainty. You have accepted the chaos in not knowing what you are doing or where you are going, and that security in the sense you have always aspired to is really an illusion. It is a difficult lesson to learn. But forced to trust that 'something will turn up', you are led eventually towards a new kind of security. The more insecure you become on the outside, the more you must find security from within.

"You can only live by habit if you go to sleep in yourself," says Lynice. "And the more you try to wake up, the more you have got to get away from that." The paradox of course is that she always craved security. But whenever she was given the opportunity, in the final event she always said no. Whenever she found herself in a secure space she had to fight free. When she had the opportunity to settle down in marriage, she knew it was wrong, and that for her the difficult path was the one she had to take, and did. "I always felt my life just pushing and pushing further and further, always getting into the most difficult situations, choosing them quite wilfully. Even when I thought it was happening against my will, I realised it was my will, and given the choice I wouldn't have chosen security." She fled from security, which was not a question of running away, but a burning need to grow.

Nor was Diana's life ever very secure. From the time she went to Esalen she had no security of any kind. She was making a hundred dollars a month plus room and board, and there was certainly no future in gardening. When she left to be with John she had financial security, but no sense of rootedness. They travelled incessantly and rented flats in which to live. "Then when John became involved in his work with psychics and extra-terrestrial life systems, everything turned upside down," she says. "I learned that what was secure in terms of things you could touch and feel was only an illusion, an energy. It was so expanding and pushing on my boundaries that my limits were constantly stretched. Nothing seemed secure in my environment." Also, for four years Diana and John were separated far more than they were able to be together, which she resented and fought. "But now I look back I know that if this hadn't happened I would never have developed as a person in my own right. I would have let John be the brilliant one and devoted my life to him. I would have taken a back seat and run the home and been the woman behind the man. The more I've come out, the more I realise this is why we had to be separated."

Gobal Singh said "security is living on another's terms which an insecure mind imposes on itself, afraid of being too much alive." It seems we must give up our need for security before we are allowed to have it. Security within allows the dance around us. Security outside can prevent that dance. We always look for security 'out there', but this is moving as well and so still we feel insecure. Security is being on your own path. There is no fixed point except within ourselves. The dance of life is within us as it relates to the world outside us. There is only the dance. We must have the courage to know that security is an illusion, that the only fixed point is death. But needing outside security is different from wanting it. We may still have roots and of course these are important. It is simply that we must be prepared to lose those roots in order to find the security within us. "Strangely," says Diana, "since I finally learned that lesson, John and I have not been separated any more. This happened exactly when I realised I had grown up as an individual in my own right and didn't need John as a prop. It was almost a shock."

The world is constantly renewing. The real present in which we live is the unknown in the process of becoming known. Like spring, the god figure bursts out saying 'look I am doing a new thing, can't you see it?' Like the plants and the trees, we each have our own cycles of growth. We are part of the rhythm of life, of the expansion and contraction of the natural world. We should rub away the mist from our image in the lake and see our true selves and our own changing patterns. The seed planted in winter expands by metamorphosis of the inner plant to produce the buds in spring. It expands again to form leaves and flowers which blossom in the summer. The seed then falls back into the ground to begin its cycle of growth again. A bamboo shoot shows perfectly this constant expansion and contraction. We too have continuing cycles within cycles of expansion and contractions of waking and sleeping. We have constant experience of death and rebirth through each stage of our lives.

Life moves and it is static, it is good and bad, it gives pain and joy, dark and light. The universe itself is a relation between spirit and matter. Every function of life is a relation between a polarity: between conscious and unconscious, love and hate, birth and death. In every aspect of our lives we are at the same time its opposite. We cannot be one without the other. We are villain and hero together. If one thing is true then the opposite is also true. To be identified too closely with one extreme is automatically to evoke the other. When the ends of a piece of string are joined to complete a circle, the one extreme sits next to the other.

To move towards wholeness we must constantly move towards our opposite in one way or another, and life is spent in constant struggle towards the balance of these opposites at every level, during every cycle of our evolution. A thrust towards "ordering our random disorderliness." Most important, we should balance our inner and outer selves, our reason or intellect, and our imagination or intuition. Life itself is a dialogue between the intellect and the imagination. If we become totally involved in one we fail to see the other. The intellect is informed by the imagination.

But we in the West have become too one-sided because our education relates only to the intellect. The human personality has body, mind, emotions and intuition to express itself and neither one is enough on its own. Our system of education trains the body a little, but primarily it trains the mind, and our emotions are virtually ignored; they are much less well integrated. Intuition, if it happens at all, will only come at certain moments. Most of us therefore have become lopsided because we are only working relatively efficiently through two aspects of our nature. To become a mature adult these enclosed areas must be opened up. It is only by strengthening the ego personality that we can clear the channel which enables us to move freely into something far bigger. The 'Self' is trying to come into expression through our daily lives, through our personality, which is the only vehicle we have to live on this earth.

Fortunately the psyche is a marvellous self-balancing mechanism. When we are in danger of becoming too lopsided it produces crises in our lives to tell us that this is so. By making us feel that life as it is, is miserable, it is holding us by the neck and telling us we must do something about it, and it won't let go until we do. (The cosmos, the macrocosm to our microcosm has its way of telling us that too). Transpersonal Psychology is a way of looking at these undeveloped aspects of the personality. It shows how to recognise the places of imbalance and how they may be set straight. It also helps to see the blocks in the personality which, in turn, block the channel to our real centre, the 'Self' that knows exactly what is right for us.

Psychosynthesis calls these problems, which on the surface seem like obstacles to our full functioning, our 'subpersonalities'. It describes them as many 'different selves' with different personalities that live inside us and show themselves according to the way we behave in different surroundings with different people. Each of these subpersonalities inside us has its own behaviour patterns, and most of the inner wars that go on are to do with the different selves wanting and needing conflicting things. Perhaps we have a 'little girl' inside us who is hungry to be loved and is jealous of everyone else. Or we may have an 'angry young man' who is spoiling for war. One subpersonality may want to live in the country, another in town. One is afraid, another full of pride.

They are all like different parts of an orchestra with each instrument playing its own tune, trying to make itself heard. Obviously the result is chaos. The orchestra needs a conductor to look at and organise the whole. When the cacophony is too loud to bear we are forced into learning to harmonise these aspects of our personality so that we may become the conductor of our own orchestra. By recognising these subpersonalities, then accepting them and finding out what they need, they can be integrated into the structure of our personality. It is a wonderful relief to realise that we are free to choose what we need and want.

No subpersonality is completely bad, but if we identify too closely with any one of them and become that personality, then that part is controlling and ruling us, and the rest of our being is not available to us. It is also consoling to know when the going gets tough, that we are never all wrong, that only parts of us are wrong.

At any moment one or two subpersonalities may be operating in the foreground and we must try to see what conflicts are trying to be resolved. When the crisis hits, we are forced into deep self-analysis which is not without a great deal of pain. Lorraine did the work herself. Once she gained intellectual coherence she found that because at last she could stand up and explain her emotions, they could become integrated. Diana, on the other hand, who trained in Psychosynthesis with Assagioli, discovered that to train with him meant to work on herself. She fought her tangled emotions through Psychosynthesis techniques.

Liz did a lot of work on herself but finally also sought help. When she had her peak experience at nineteen, her mind and intuition were obviously functioning well. It was her physical and emotional life which wreaked havoc. The only aspect of her that worked was her intellect, which is what she used to survive. She made it her defence. It was emotionally that she was crippled. She desperately wanted to love and be loved, to have an emotional rapport with someone so that she didn't feel so completely cut off. But every relationship she had fell to pieces. "I have had a very colourful past! I just went mad. It was like having a beast on a leash beside me which kept dragging loose. I couldn't control it. I couldn't understand why I was burdened with this kind of intense emotional nature, which had a life of its own and which went where it pleased and shattered everything else." She didn't know how this fitted into her knowing. She wanted detachment from her emotions because they were so tormenting, but she fell obsessively in love no matter with whom it was.

Because of her relationship with her father she was attracted to weak or brutal men; she could only see men as one or the other. She had never acquired the instinctive feminine side of her nature through which a girl learns how to be a woman. At seventeen or eighteen she developed a drive for power and was determined not to submit to that kind of relationship. Because her mother had been unable to teach her the pleasant side of femininity, she remained a masked child looking for affection. "If I attracted men as a vamp, they didn't understand the child," she says. "I couldn't become the feminine side. If I fell for someone I fell hard and then after a few weeks the jockeying for power began again. I'd walk in and out of relationships with no intention of loving."

Despite the traumas she had remained at university and managed to take her Ph.D. She knew she had to have this 'ridiculous piece of paper' or a great many doors would have been closed to her. But she knew she would have failed except for that one particular tutor who saw potential in her and helped her through the course. During her first marriage she felt isolated. She was prickly and introverted and suspicious of people. She knows she seemed cold to anyone who met her. "When I left college and spent that first summer in New York, I made friends with junkies, dope pushers and hookers. It was almost as if there was some kind of relationship there which I couldn't have with peers, the people I was supposed to be friends with. I went through some of the drug scene – LSD and grass, no hard drugs – but it bored me. I wanted to get out of my isolation, I wanted something that would make me feel better but which didn't negate my knowing."

She seemed to have done everything back to front. People were seeking spiritual experience which she had had, but she had no one with whom to communicate what she had experienced, and they seemed in better shape than she was. They talked a great deal about it but couldn't understand it. She had experienced it but couldn't live it. She tried everything to find some help with her emotional life. She had experienced Freudian psychology as part of her training, but learning about her parents' reactions didn't realease the pain.

Her work in astrology was something quite different. She devoured this in the same way she did anything to which she was passionately attracted. As long as she was fulfilling that part she had something to hang on to. As an astrologer and counsellor she was always 'sane enough to work with people'. But what was the use of knowing that there was a point and purpose to life if she couldn't relate to herself as a woman? By this time she had made herself secure in her career and become so immersed in work that she was almost convinced she had come through the emotional blocks, because all she did was work. But there came a point at which she knew she couldn't live like that any more. She couldn't continue to violate her instinctive nature and feelings, particularly since she had now met Ian, and intuition told her that this was a very different relationship. Unlike most of the men she had fallen for, this wasn't her father. "I came to the decision that I had to have further analysis of a different kind and that is when I was introduced to Jungian psychology. Now I know how I was being affected by my father's unconscious, I have some peace."

These 'obstacles' to our well-being, our fears, our un-fulfilled desires, our violent emotions and frustrations are considered to be 'sins' in our modern psychiatric 'religion'. But Transpersonal Psychology says that these problems may instead be used – chosen even – by us to give form and colour to our personalities. Our problems may be used as tools to develop in consciousness. Problems are a process of life and help us to move and change. We do not need to be free of problems, but by facing them and saying, yes that belongs to me, we take away their power. We can choose not to use them unless in a certain situation it is right to. Then we can make them work *for* us, not against us. According to psychosynthesis, every problem is regulated by the 'higher Self' to pull the personality on to a certain path. Even physical illness does this.

Our problems may be seen as a blessing. "One of the troubles with humanity," says Diana, "is avoidance of pain. so much of our life and energy is spent in avoiding being hurt and creating situations so we don't experience anything bad. Western medicine is guilty of that too."

All of us have different roles to fulfill and different tasks to perform. The individual path is suited to that task. Liz couldn't work with the personal wrecks as clients if she hadn't been a wreck herself. She could never have understood what they were going through, or how alone a person can be, if she hadn't felt that loneliness herself. "I think my place is in the dark and I love the darkness in people. I couldn't get down in that muck if I hadn't been as used to it as I am."

It occurs to Lynice more and more that she didn't take the LSD by chance. It was to be her particular path to cope with the resulting chaos and inner mess. At the home in Gloucestershire where she worked as housemother to maladjusted children before going on to Emerson College, she immediately got on well. She had no problem with discipline. Yet although it gave her confidence to do something where people respected her, she was ill most of the time. The children were so volatile that, aggravated by the psychic experiences caused by the LSD, the emotional strain was catastrophic. It came to the point eventually where she was on the verge of a nervous break-down. She couldn't cope any more. "It was the biggest crisis of my life," she says. "I thought I was going mad." But then, in one of those synchronistic meetings, she met a woman who introduced her to Curative Eurythmy and she began to see that help was coming for her to weather this storm. "I began to perceive I wasn't on my own."

At Emerson College, where she learned more about Steiner's work, obviously she met people who were going through a similar kind of crisis. At once she felt like someone who had been starved. At last she had people to talk to and a true knowledge to guide her. It was a student at Emerson helped her particularly to understand the relevance of what had happened to her through the LSD and who taught her to be glad for the crises in her life. He had been through similar experiences, even worse than her own, and he showed her that she would have to go through these crises because this is how you do it. She accepted it for the first time in her life.

At Emerson, too, they discussed about people who chose to come to earth to go into the most difficult situations in order to grow. "And I can see this happening," she says. "There are some people who have to have bad times because only through knowing them in yourself can you help other people. I feel with my class that I am destined to be with this group of children. I know I am their teacher and it is very obvious between us. I can see now that I have something to give them because of what I have been through. Because I have pulled myself up out of the blackness and despair and I have something to offer other people."

To an astrologer, it is the Saturn cycle that indicates the major crisis points in our lives. Saturn is said to have seven year trigger points and roughly every seven years we seem to feel its effect. Since its influence is usually felt from the year before and continues to affect us until the year after, a cycle spans approximately three yearrs. The third time Saturn impinges on an individual, at around the age of twenty-one, seems to be particularly important and appears to link up with the following cycle. At the age of twenty-nine Saturn returns to the exact place it occupied in the horoscope at the moment of birth. The main impact on our lives can be felt then. It is at this point that everything digested during the other three trigger points comes up again and we are given the opportunity to try to make use of all these experiences and to make them conscious. The area of life in which these changes become apparent depends on where Saturn falls in a birthchart, but almost invariably it seems to mean a rumbling and grinding and breaking down, the eruption of difficulties of one kind or another. People find they express it in different ways, but these mean the same thing. The energy released in the psyche is utilised according to the quality of the instrument. There are big awakenings or little ones depending on who you are, but change is inevitable. The hard hit at around twenty-nine gives us the chance to lay to rest all the childhood ghosts and all our parental identification, the things we have become caught up in and accepted into our personality but which really have nothing to do with us. We then have the opportunity to repossess our true selves and take responsibility for our own lives. In other words, to grow up.

In classical astrology, any progression to Saturn, Uranus or Pluto, particularly if the progression moves through difficult aspects in opposition or conjunction, is seen to mean conflict. Any progressed planet hitting these three or the transit of any of them over an important area of the birth chart gives plenty of opportunity for people to kick over the traces and emerge from the castle they have built up around themselves. They symbolise different kinds of death, in relationships or work, or an identity crisis. Something in the ego has to die. They mean an incredible awakening in which one might fall in love or be creative for the first time. The Saturn hits at roughly twenty-one and twenty-eight years give us ample opportunity to take the plunge and begin to realise the unexplored parts of ourselves. Unconsciously the coincidences present us with people or situations that can take us into areas we need to go.

The affect of each hit depends on how well we handled the last one. If we consolidate well at thirty, there is room for change at forty but this is usually more positive. There is a further hit at the age of forty-two when Uranus is opposite its natal place. This provokes what Jung called the 'mid-life crisis' which begins its build-up at the thirty-five year hit. Between thirty and forty everything that hasn't been given the opportunity to move comes flying out, and in the same way that the meaning of the twenty-one hit becomes clear at twenty-eight, the meaning of the turning point at thirty-five becomes clear around forty-two. At any of these hits one can begin to flower and almost always an inferior function is given the opportunity to develop. If you have always worked with your intellect, you may suddenly, like Gauguin, become an artist.

The continuing need for security makes most people identify with a role. We are a mother or a wife or a career woman or businessman. While we play the role, it keeps us safe. But when for some reason we realise that we are not this character, a tremendous crisis of identity can occur. If I am not a mother or an executive, who am I? When Isobel came to London she knew she had come as far as she could in her profession. By assuming the nurse's uniform she had made herself the sort of woman who is capable of fulfilling whatever role is demanded of her. She did not question her mental abilities because she always knew she could give people what they expected; this was her survival mechanism. In exams she knew how to give what was expected of her even though often this wasn't necessarily what she would normally have said or done. It worked well. "I remember in one exam the doctor said he had no option but to give me a hundred per cent although it had never been done before. But I knew it wasn't a matter of what I knew".

Yet when she arrived in England she had no idea of herself as a person. She had no understanding of her emotional nature. She doubted herself as a woman and had no idea of her abilities in relating to a man. She simply didn't know what was expected when it came to relationships. Then she met Alex. "The average man would have given me a role and I would quickly have learned to fill it. But he wasn't the sort of man to have expectations of me, and I was lost because he didn't give me a role. I kept wanting to know what was expected so I could do that. If I didn't know, how could I do it?" She was insecure because she couldn't understand. She was trying to work out what the game was all the time, but he was always a couple of jumps ahead of her. She had great fear of doing the wrong thing because if she did it she thought she would be rejected. "In fact I was having to learn to trust myself with nobody around to guide me. By not giving me a role he gave me a lot of trust in myself as a woman and did a lot to build up confidence and accept my own state of being. Somehow I managed to come through."

Quite often in the beginning we have to learn to play these roles to build up our confidence, but if we take the roles seriously, we can become stuck in them. To grow and come closer to our truer selves we must dissociate ourselves from the roles we play. Not to stop playing them altogether but to recognise them for what they are in order to learn to use them effectively and to choose them objectively when we need them to enhance our life and personality. Once we use the roles through choice and aren't stuck inside them, we can then learn to play them even better. Similarly, there is danger in people choosing a system of belief or path of growth and then getting caught up in the form.

Balancing never stops. It is a continuing process of waking up, a constant motion within those cycles of change. Being is perpetually becoming, we are bound in a world of becoming. Opposites must marry or there will be no change. Yet, paradoxically, if the opposites remain balanced then this too is to be stuck. All opposites are resolved in a unity, a gradual synthesis, but that balance must not freeze. As Stevens says in 'Order at Key West', there is no resolution in two ideas, except when they make a momentary order. As soon as you freeze it, you have nothing to renew. A fixed image cannot satisfy the imagination which is an 'irrepressible revolutionist'.

As soon as we are setting down the last experience, we are embarking on the next. And within those cycles the pattern repeats become clear. We have set up our problems to give our personality some shape and we spend our lives working with these problems. We deal with them on one level and they are over for a while. Then they pop up again on a more refined level. The circle of change becomes a spiral. We feel we have regressed but we have not. What we are has to be developed and refined. What arrives has to be added to what we are, and then that has to go up too to be developed and refined. Evolution is adding to what is and it goes on forever. Our true self is working towards resolution between the basic human polarity; the human personality as a whole and the spiritual self. The process involves conflicts and contact; each time pushing forward to an increasingly expanded unity. "Spiritual psychosynthesis is the central drama of man who either consciously or unconsciously aspires to this goal or is pushed towards it to find true peace," says Assagioli.

We must balance the terror of being man with the wonder of being man.

It must give Pleasure

"And round and round, the merely going round,
Until merely going round is a final good,
The way wine comes at a table in a wood."

Wallace Stevens *Notes Towards A Supreme Fiction*

Survival. This is the issue for most of us. A fight to like oneself. Survival begins by shutting off the things we don't like, by taking on roles and 'acting as if', and by making projections, which is another way of unconsciously hiding the cause of the odd things that happen. A projection is happening when, for example, you think you are a good, even-tempered person but in fact have repressed a dislike for someone else, and then when a quarrel occurs you are certain it was the other person who started it. A projection has a very powerful effect on the person on whom you are projecting. You can't project if he doesn't have an underlying dislike for you buried somewhere in him, but when you unconsciously project your dislike on to him, you feed the dislike lying dormant in him, and cause him to react in that way. Projection makes relationships very difficult.

Liking yourself comes gradually as you begin to bolster up the parts you do like and set the Will in motion to come to terms with the parts you don't. But as you become more fully integrated in every aspect you are taking back the entire responsibility for your being. This is the process of growing up. It is a hit and miss affair, a hotchpotch of stages which, except for the rare few, tend to come completely out of sequence. A process set in motion through crises and conflict and fraught with trauma. "It is a naive misunderstanding," says Lorraine, "to assume that anyone who has convictions didn't have some doubts and terrors. All of us should understand that in basic humanity life cannot be supportive all the time. Any commitment means you have to select moments away from people and that means pain, to you and to those people. There is also pain in terms of effort."

The pain is particularly acute at the beginning of the cycle that surrounds a peak experience. Thrown into an isolated sea from which it seems impossible to communicate, you sense you have been set apart from the rest of the world through some special higher awareness, but it hurts. You don't quite know yourself what you know. All you do know is that the rest of the world doesn't seem to know it. But the other side of that coin is pleasure. Where there is the deepest pain there is also the greatest joy. Alongside the confusion comes the certainty of that energy and its tremendous surge for good.

Eventually when the circle returns to itself and the cycle is complete, you must return to the space you left. Except for a qualitative change you can return to life as you knew it before. After all the fire and fury it is a relief to come back to being 'ordinary' again. If you don't you are stuck in an unreal world. You return with consciousness which enriches the quality of life many many times but it is still the same thing. "It taught me respect for people who I once judged unconscious," says Liz. "We are all male or female with the same sense organs, living the same life with the same drives and desires. It is only that this experience gives greater insights." For Lynice this consciousness invested life with something much greater than she had ever conceived of. It gave her the sense that what she could see happening around her was a very small manifestation of something she couldn't see. It made her stop judging things superficially, taking them at face value.

On a practical level it forced her to push her horizons and discover something more in herself. She had always admired the artists and creative people with whom she was brought into contact, and these were the people who meant something to her. Yet she would constantly feel inadequate, wishing to be an artist but wondering why she didn't have any of the wonderful talent they had. "Slowly over the years I have discovered talents inside me which I never dreamed were there," she says. "I feel that they have always been inside me fighting to come out, but have been covered by layers of fog. They are gradually coming to light now and it was as though I had to meet these people to bring them out." Once the cycle is complete, the exaggeration of pain and joy becomes more balanced. "Obviously there are times when you get fed up," says Lynice. "But teaching children is sheer joy. I love having a class of children to whom I can bring things. Their enthusiasm and pleasure is very rewarding."

Liking of self does not mean liking in a separative, personal sense or in an egocentric way that craves pleasure and possessiveness. This sense of a link with something bigger somehow suggests love on a much wider level. "My vision made me aware of myself as a being," says Lorraine. "It was as though my position on the planet was affirmed and I felt a consuming love in the sense of being aware of my worth and consequently of everyone else's." Of course the personal self still needs care and attention, but there is a qualitative change. Running parallel to this personal concern is the urge to live in a very positive, non-wasteful way, because now you know that every individual has a powerful psychological influence on the environment. We each have a personal responsibility. Just as it is increasingly important to understand the dangers of polluting the ecological environment, we need also to be aware of the psycho-ecological environment too. It is our responsibility to produce the 'good vibrations'.

For Diana the quality of that knowing was love. She could always see beauty in everyone but this was a feeling of inclusiveness, that each human being is as important as the next. Her feeling of love was inspired by the dissonance between knowing what she did and knowing what man has become today; and that dissonance activated her more. It gave her the desire to change it. If all of us set our will towards personal synthesis, we could deal with the negative within us and around us. We could gain protection from the internal poisons by converting them into harmless or even useful foods. The problem today, Assagioli said, is a lack of love on the part of those who have will and lack of will on the part of those who have love. The link with Self is a step towards integrating love and will.

Self-absorption is a danger, of course, but this has to happen at some stage to find out about yourself. You must then find the strength to pull out of it. "When I was at Emerson I often felt dissatisfied and self-absorbed, trying to solve inner problems," says Lynice. "But when I came to Bristol and was confronted with so many unhappy people, with terrible problems, it pulled me out of myself with a jerk. I've never been able to feel sorry for myself since." We all go through stages of selfishness, but the stronger the link with the 'Higher Self', the less the personal self matters. The impulse then is to 'serve' and it becomes unselfish. The possessiveness of insecurity goes, and with it the need for attachments to people or ideas that often leads to excess and greed and an ignorance of the wholeness of being.

Friendships seem easier because the games normally played become unnecessary. An irritation with other people is often simply reaction against the things we don't like in ourselves. By accepting yourself, others will accept you too. If you, your own severest critic, say you're all right, then others can think so too. If you recognise your own space, you have no need to invade someone else's privacy. Being truly yourself has tremendous power, there is nothing that you cannot achieve. Confidence evokes confidence from others and draws people in need towards it for support. It acts as a catalyst for other people's change. Of course the liking and sureness of self ebbs and flows as it always did; evolution is not one straight progression. But the knowing – that core of consciousness – remains, and it is this that others will unconsciously recognise.

The more insecure or unconscious, the more we need relationships to tell us who we are. As you grow and integrate the whole of your being, the sense of who you are grows too. By standing back and being yourself, you allow the other person to do the same. Because you do not need to project yourself on to anyone else, there will be empathy at a distance. "The distance might seem greater," says Isobel, "but in fact I can come much closer to people in my work. I relate to people much more fully now than I did before when I was trying to relate from my own insecurities. Now I am trying to be myself, I allow them to be themselves. The more objective you are, the more subjective you can be. I can become more emotionally involved but also extricate myself more quickly."

Diana, too, would be unable to do the work she does if she became emotionally involved with her clients. "Now when I look at the pain of men and women, I no longer see their pain as bad," she says. "I don't want to put Bandaid on their cuts, and if someone cries I don't gushingly try to make it better. Now in a crisis I step back and say 'that's good, they are growing'."

In some ways this freedom may also be a threat. If someone, particularly a woman, is very sure of her pace and the rightness of her freedom of spirit, this can be frightening to other people. They recognise something they are not ready to take on for themselves. In a love relationship particularly, it takes a special kind of partner to understand this kind of inner strength and the need for a freedom which is totally different from permissiveness. It is, in fact, a greater commitment, not less. When it does work, the quality of love in a relationship is greatly changed. "Whatever you say, it sounds trite," says Lynice, "but love, when one feels good with another person and gets that high feeling, is usually self-satisfaction. Being in love is totally giving. For me love is an experience of a very real cosmic force to do with the force of the Christ, which is something we haven't nearly begun to understand yet."

Until she went to Esalen, Diana says, her love was always very distorted because she was so insecure. She always hated new relationships with men, which she had about every six months. She hated the adjustment, particularly at the beginning. All her relationships used to be based on mutual need, each feeding the other's hangups. "This is the difference between a mature realised relationship and an unrealised one," she says. "Between deep spiritual love and superficial emotional love." Personal love is possessive. It is an egotistical love, the love of being loved. "Many people when they say 'I love you' mean 'I want you to love me'. Even being with John I had this, but love begins to move from the personal to a spiritual kind of love. A love that wants what is best for that person. This is what loving them means. Now love is wanting for the other person, but it is also saying, you're standing on my foot, get off, I love you. I now recognise what I need as well as what the other person needs."

Throughout life people 'turn up' at the most crucial moments to act as catalysts for change. It may be a passing meeting or become a firm friendship. Of course men or women can be instrumental in sparking off illuminations or providing inspiration, but radical changes, particularly for women, often seem to come through love. The 'rightness' of a relationship that turned up at the time of the peak experience for each of these women brought a conscious recognition that this man was of special importance at this particular stage. The relationship might not necessarily last, but it was important to be together at this time to be mutual teachers.

As soon as Diana met John, to whom she is now married, she knew in spite of the doubts and difficulties that she was meant to be with him. They are opposite in all ways: he a Will type, she emotional; he dynamic, she quiet and introverted. But they both recognise a strength gained through each other. They have been given the opportunity to develop their opposite sides. "Before I met John I didn't want to know about mind and books. Through both John and Assagioli I began to develop my mind." By being apart so much Diana learned a lot about being strong and assertive, about 'recognising who I am'. Even though they don't work together they feel they have a similar direction and that their paths are just different branches of the same path, and this has surprised them. They both grew and changed so much by being together, it is remarkable to think that they made it. "But we both feel it has something to do with having been together in past lives, which is a sense I have always had with

John," she says. "It is just a knowing, like the familiarity I experienced in the meeting with Assagioli, which felt like coming home. I know I have been with him a lot in the past and this is what held us together through all the despair – even when we were ready to say we're not making it and had no reason nor rational purpose to stay together and neither of us knew why we did."

The special man in each case seems to have moved the woman into areas of herself which she had been unable to reach before. When Isobel met Alex she knew he was exactly who she needed in that they too were opposites. "I think my head was full of nonsense about relationships and he cut through that in a down-to-earth kind of way. In his amazing understanding and widom he had this ability to see what is really there and not get tangled with the superficial. He widened my vision tremendously." In trying to understand and relate to the opposite she was led into an enormous amount of growth.

It also appears that once he has acted as a catalyst the man must leave for one reason or another – sometimes for good, sometimes not – to allow the woman to continue this growth and find security within herself. Tony was the first person who ever really listened to Lorraine, and recognised that she might have intuitive instincts that were paranormal. He was the only person patient enough to tell her that it was all right to be inarticulate, because she basically understood what the words meant, even if she couldn't express herself. He taught her how to put her feelings into words and was also the first person to push her back into painting and so back into her purpose. He pushed her to change, but because he was so secure in himself, he also became her security. Finally she knew she must leave him in order to gain her own inner strength by living alone with her work.

Love also acted as a catalyst for Lynice and proved to be a major turning point. "It was nothing like I have ever experienced in my life, a strong spiritual force. It just wasn't what love has ever mant to me before. It was too powerful to sustain at that stage of my development but it transformed my whole life and I've been a totally different person since then. It suddenly made the knowledge I had deeper, and I am certain he was sent to show me how to cope with my life. He taught me to fight."

Ian, on the other hand, is not opposite to Liz because they are both predominantly intuitive people. Nor did he have to go away. But since she has always found it easier to leave a relationship than to stay with it, Ian represented an opposite in the sense that he presented a situation from which she couldn't run. Because of her love for him she had to stay and work things through, to get some kind of understanding with him. "It didn't trigger an opposite exactly," she says, "but a tremendous growth."

There is a link between sex and the spiritual path which may have relevance to the confusion and unhappiness that surrounds sex today. Sexual problems have reached almost epidemic proportions and of course the reasons are multiple and complex and will continue to be discussed for ever. But much of it arises out of the confusion in women's sexual role. One generation tells women to wait until marriage and then to lie back and tolerate sex. The next generation says marry before you enjoy sex. The next says love before you enjoy it and the next generation says just enjoy it. We have become so perplexed that we are not quite sure what to enjoy any more. Consequently we try to do what other people, encouraged by the media, suggest we should do. If women accept the current opinion that they are equal in all ways to men, they are provoked into believing that their instincts should behave like those of men. And men, in their own confusion, believe this too, but they also expect women to have all the other attitudes at the same time. No wonder we are all confused! We begin not to know what love or marriage or sex are in these categorised but arbitrary terms. Thus sex breaks down all round and relationships don't work.

Sexual permissiveness will never be the answer. Promiscuity in women is often the manifestation of frigidity. It is only a reaction to confusion. Sex is relationship, and women particularly, do need a meaningful union. When it doesn't happen there are problems. And what can happen when sex is a problem is that the energy which would normally be used to drive that instinctive function, is sublimated to a spiritual level. In other words, forced upwards. This will happen more often in women because it is they who have the greater confusion between relationship and performance of the physical act. Some women might have to reach a spiritual consciousness and understand this, before they can return to function as a woman. If they do so, sex takes on a qualitative change. Liz has said she did everything back to front. Where most women carry out their instinctual function in the first half of their lives and go on to the creative part, she was forced to live it the other way round. She had no idea how to function as a female until after she saw the relevance of the spiritual. In the esoteric language of spiritual teaching, there is said to be a connection between the sex chakra or energy centre in the body, and that of the creative energy centre. As we evolve the energy moves up from the instinctual sex centre to that of creativity. This is true of all artists who seem either to have periods of fervent sexual activity or a burst of creativity.

For anyone who begins on a spiritual path the sex drives and energy tend to lessen, says Diana. Her clients get worried that they are frigid or impotent, but this is an organic part of the process. "John and I have found enormous changes in our sex attitudes. I was never a sexy lady, I couldn't make love without a deep love, but of course John was a normal male. Now that has changed dramatically. We don't make love as often but the union we experience is more spiritually oriented. Even when John and I were not together I didn't want sex because my energy and consciousness were focused on my work, on service. We still have that. When both of us are creative and involved in our work that energy moves up." Sex *can* be a physical manifestation of union with God, a symbolic union on our earthly level. In a truly equal partnership between two people sex can be the ultimate way of bringing the spiritual down to earth; of balancing the polarity between spirit and matter. But the tragedy of our society is that people who are not sexually oriented are told they have something wrong with them – which happens to many women – when this is clearly not true.

The more secure we become inside ourselves, the less we need to be dependent on external forces. We can impose flexible routines and structures on ourselves rather than labour under those from outside. Under our own responsible control we can even be more controlled than we are when outside influences are trying to control us. Ultimately there can be no real authority except in obeying oneself. This is not anarchy but personal responsibility. Present politics cannot answer our needs.

We have changed more in the last two hundred years since the Industrial Revolution than we did over the whole period from around 2000 BC. From that time the individual has increasingly lost his joy in work as a manifestation of his being. He is now completely isolated from the satisfaction of seeing the product of his labour as a whole. Capitalism is greedy. It is egocentric. The object of capitalist productivity is consumption. We are bullied to consume more and more. Our desires are stimulated and our appetites grow. To acquire becomes the dominant drive. Our present use of the earth's resources is wasteful and expensive. We plunder the planet and the resources are not replaced. Capitalism is concerned with standard of living, not the quality of life. With sheer consumerism this lopsidedness of the ego becomes spiritual poverty. No wonder people are becoming disillusioned.

At the other extreme of political thinking Marxists talk about the love of the individual human being. Because modern workers don't own the goods they produce, they are alienated from the product of their labour. The answer to this alienation, they say, is for the worker to control his own means of production. But this impersonal idea of love has led to dogma. Marx' theory was that a society will develop until all possible ways of production are used up, to the point where, when all the forces are in operation, the way of production becomes a contradiction. Then there will be revolution. The dominant economic class will be overthrown by the class dominated, and a new class formed. Feudalism was the domination of the peasantry by landlords and middle classes. When feudalism had had its day, and was hanging back the economy, the bourgeoisie overthrew the landlords. A capitalist state, Marx said, will develop to the point where capitalism is a contradiction and there will be a revolt. He talked about class in two senses. The proletarian mass, the workers, are a class, but for a class to take action it must make the transition from being a class in itself to become a class for itself. When contradictions in capitalism occur, the workers will become a class for themselves and there will be revolution. To begin with there will be a dictatorship of workers because society will still have bourgeois elements which must be eliminated, but after an unspecified amount of time, society will have eliminated landed aristocracy and become a society of one class. There will be workers only, a classless society that can make the transition from socialism to communism. This, said Marx, is inevitable. It is only the matter of timing of the contradictions. The principle function of the state, he said was at best to mediate, at worst to dominate, and when there was a classless society there was no function for the state. The state will disappear when we have a classless society.

Marx presented a dogmatic assumption in his model of history, and at the same time he stressed the dialectical nature of truth. But the fact that he insisted on the impossibility of absolute truth, has been forgotten. Marx said that the workers must be educated for revolution, and that this would come when the proletariat was a class for itself and as a politically conscious mass, could arise. When Lenin arrived he said that the masses were still ignorant and were not going to become poltically mature overnight, so the Communist Party must lead the masses. Russia still has dictatorship of workers by the Party. And the lofty ideal of 'liberation' seems to mean control of a country, not freedom of the individual from drudgery and alienation and exploitation. All the countries where revolution has taken place have been economically backward and have had to be taken rapidly into health. This might arguably have been done faster under capitalism.

The most relevant point is that Marx also said that society makes man. He did not accept that man makes society and that self-development cannot be imposed from above or forced from outside. For him the answer was in changing the world itself, imposing the perfect system by force. He did say that the perfect society needed the highest spiritual nature of man to be used in creation of that society, but that materialism would call up the highest spiritual nature of man. This must be a fundamental contradiction. Our problem is of the individual on the one hand and of society on the other, and of the interaction betweenthe two. At the moment it is up to the individual.

Capitalism in the West is egotistical; but we have seen that the natural progression from self-actualisation is towards self-realisation. Our quest in the West should now be for a return from the material towards the spiritual. Increasingly we become aware that the planet cannot survive until we change our consciousness. Our destruction of the planet, a process which has been accelerating alarmingly over the last few years, brings more and more pressure to bear on individuals to get themselves into a new framework of thinking. It is almost as if the collective force is thrusting us all forward. The light of the world is shining very brightly and showing up the huge imperfections in the vehicle. Now is a time for do or die. As Isobel says, "If I can be whole myself, then I am already helping society by producing one individual less to worry about. And it is as if by being as whole as possible in myself I can influence other people to be whole."

Unless you change the basic underlying attitude of the people, you cannot change the forms in which society operates. If you are working towards becoming responsible as an individual, society will automatically change.

3

Innocence and Experience

*"This is the stage of ourselves
now. Divorced from innocence,
as yet undirected by intuition,
man walks a bridge between these
two states of grace."*

Michael Adam in *Man is a Little World*

Education

*"Education is an originally implied,
eductive, the communication of
wisdom that leads man out of his chrysalis into
unity with his fellow man."*

Martin Buber

Children have innocence. Naive, unsophisticated and obli-
vious to the effects of modern living, they live close to nature.
Unaware of time itself – or of death – children have a natural
trust of things and of people. They are guileless and
irrational, with a constantly fresh view of things around
them. They see instinctively, with the innocent eye. Children
are unified, not divided. They have what adults have
somehow lost. But innocence dwells in wisdom, never with
ignorance. Fools won't enter the Kingdom of Heaven, said
Blake. To live by instinct means to respond naturally to the
laws of nature, to enter spontaneously into the rhythm of life.
To know unconsciously the rightness of life and that man is
living at one with the universe. We are born with the wisdom
of the sage. A child knows everything.

In the mythology of every culture, it is the creation myths
that speak about the state of innocence. These archetypes
appear in myths and religions, in the dreams we have, in
fiction of all kinds. They are simply dressed up in different
ways like separate characters in a slightly original story. They

are images from the collective unconscious, the storehouse of everything that anyone has ever known and to which we all have access, and are the fundamental source of the energy of the human psyche. They are a common pool of images with which we make symbolic connections. With the instinct of children the old storytellers believed in the marvels of myth, in the stories of strange, powerful creatures and the wonders of magic. But with the spread of education and the materialistic civilisation these stories are now considered to be nothing but superstition. We have lost our innocence.

But myths are made up out of the inner happenings of humanity, and in the universal theme of mythology the hero soon abandons childish things. He is challenged to begin a search or make a journey into other worlds, into the world of heroines and enchantments, of ogres and monsters. His seriousness is tested by warnings in the form of an ugly person. But the hero accepts the challenge and by doing so is prepared to leave all natural ties. He is thrown into a period of fear and shrinking into a pattern of chaos, with nature around him often in as great a turmoil as he is.

A child must leave his state of innocence in order to grow. A child is full of his own potential. He is the carrier of the seed which wishes to develop in this one lifetime. There is never another seed like it, and our potential is to be worked through. For Self is what life is all about. Self leading life through the personality. To begin our journey towards consciousness we must understand our own individuality. Weaving through our own enchantments and ogres, we must first become aware of our ego consciousness. We carry a lot of unknown material within us, and throughout life we are working to become awakened. Since each man reflects the whole of humanity and is the microcosm of the macrocosm, it follows that humanity must know itself consciously too. Western man through his materialistic growth has been evolving towards the point of ego consciousness. Humanity has been acquiring its personality. But in order to find this consciousness man has had to withdraw from the spiritual. The fall of Adam showed man the double values of life between which he had to thread his way. Genesis is the representation of the coming of self-consciousness and the confrontation humanity would have to face.

But man has not quite lost sight of his origins. The conflict of scientific rationalism and instinctive faith is seldom completely resolved in any of us. It constantly presents us with prejudices and inconsistencies, and at the height of our materialism we begin again to be aware of the deep significance of realities that cannot be fully explained in categories of reason, or understood by history and science. It is an awareness that has always proved an inexhaustible fount of inspiration for poets and artists.

Never in myth is the hero totally defeated. He opens up to the warmth of success, and ultimately has the strength to be what life has made him. Once he has accepted that challenge a hero cannot go back. He cannot do anything other than that he has done. He accepts that it is out of death that life arises. We cannot go back on our culture. We needed our materialistic approach to become fully conscious. Evolution must continue through the things we already have. We cannot forget what we know and go back. It is for this reason that clinging to the old Eastern philosophies, while obviously more spiritually oriented, is not necessarily the right approach for us. They responded to a need in a non-material people and were right for them at that time. We have need to go on to renew the spirit, not to go back to the old.

If, once he has acquired his material needs, the individual goes on in his evolution to self-actualisation and on towards self-realisation with awareness of the spiritual values, then humanity can do so too. Through the pain and suffering of experience we may move on to renewed innocence. We may again find a childlike state, but through the evolutionary spiral our innocence is regained with far greater insight. We complete the spiral from instinct to intuition; from an unconscious link with the universe to a conscious knowing of that link. A child means joy, and man can move on to use again the energy of eternal delight, to use his own natural energies which have become so distorted because so badly repressed. And by returning to renewed innocence, we can learn again how to live within the community, as we once did instinctively, to live with other people in harmony and balance and for mutual benefit. From a stage of community, through a stage of the individual, and on to a new awareness of community.

Innocence cannot be appreciated until it is renewed, until it is organised. Unorganised innocence is an impossibility for adults. Renewal of the spirit comes with organised man, and each of us is struggling all our lives to organise the living force which as Eliot says 'costs no less than everything'. We need simplicity imbued with technical experience. And as Blake says, only when he returns to innocence will man be as high as he was intended to be. Only then will he be at his full potential. If only we were conscious of our process of growth, we might make easier the struggle to renewed innocence, a struggle based on a secure foundation, not on guilt or suppression or ignorance. If a child were brought up in the security of rightness there would be no need for him to fear his instinctive energies.

Lynice had virtually rejected civilisation at the community in Corsica. The university system depressed her. The thought of people just wanting jobs for money because they couldn't think of anything else in life seemed pointless. Shutting yourself away is no solution. It is just a selfish act and doesn't help anyone. But how can you change the world? "It became obvious that if I wanted to contribute to the community I had to help children to grow in the right way," says Lynice. "Since society is a reflection of the people in it, you can change society through true education." She was having these thoughts when she heard about Rudolf Steiner and read his guidelines on education. It was a slow understanding, but this really began to interest her. Most schools in this country teach thinking – to think, or not to think, depending on which way you look at it. They teach us to pass exams and have a certain knowledge which helps us get on in the world and to suit certain jobs. But no concern is shown for our life of feeling, or the concept of Will – except perhaps in boarding schools where it is used in a negative way to make you tough. Steiner is different in saying that one has to educate the whole man.

In educating a child, said Steiner (1861-1925), we must know what the child is. That he is a being who has successively incarnated on earth and is born each time with different qualities in order to grow. A being who has chosen his destiny before coming to earth and who will continue to exist after his death. You cannot just pour knowledge into a child, but must recognise him as a spiritual being and educate him to carry this knowledge with him. "You must have absolute reverence for other human beings," says Lynice. "And by understanding the strong karmic connections, a teacher must fully realise the responsibility to that child. Ultimately he is responsible for himself, but for this time he has put himself in your hands and you are as responsible for his development as his parents."

Rudolf Steiner is difficult to study. It would take a whole lifetime and more to understand fully the implications of what his vision has to offer us. But, relating to the physical body, he explains precisely the spiritual forces at work in the development of the child. He is never nebulous and warns against people being so. Wonderful statements like 'being all one', mean virtually nothing. He gave precise indications of what happens to a child in his developent, of how he is actually incarnated into the body, and what spiritual forces are working within him. He gave a three-fold picture of man who carries within himself forces of thinking, feeling and willing, and how successively during the development of the child one of these forces is predominant, although of course all three interweave constantly. He showed how a child grows up through his willing, which is centred in the limbs, then into his feeling life (centred in the heart and breathing) and then into his thinking (centred in the head). At the same time the child develops physically from the head downwards. A baby has a large head and undeveloped limbs. From seven to fourteen years the rhythmic system develops and at the time of puberty the limbs now shoot out.

Steiner presented a picture of a spiritual being choosing the body he is going to inhabit and how, slowly over the years, he takes hold of that body. Steiner shows from acute observation how a very young baby lives completely in his will. A baby has no thinking, but his whole body moves expressing everything he feels. Even when the baby sucks his mother's breast, his toes are moving, expressing his whole being.

According to Steiner there are three important stages in a child's development: the first is when he stands upright, which only man does, when certain spiritual forces are flowing through him. The second is speech, the great miracle of human beings. Stage three is thinking. Unlike other psychologists, Steiner believed a child begins to develop his thinking at roughly the age of three.

The next step towards development of the child is at the age of seven when the milk teeth are lost and the real teeth grow. This, said Steiner, is a sign in the physical body that the formative forces working to shape and form the organs have actually finished the greater part of their task. They are still being used, but some may be released to be used for thinking. "You must never start educating a child in an intellectual way until that happens," says Lynice. "Otherwise you will ruin the whole bodily organisation of the child. By taking away forces that are needed for growth at this stage, there will be severe physical problems by the age of fifty. In everything we do for the child we must be aware of the effect this is having on his later life."

The age divisions can differ widely, probably because we have now lost our natural rhythm. But roughly between the ages of seven and fourteen, through puberty, the child moves up from the will forces (from the toddler who stamps his feet and says no), to the middle realm of breathing and feeling. Bearing this in mind he must now be educated through the whole feeling element. "With five year-olds you can tell the story of a farmer who fed the ducks, then milked the cows, then collected the eggs – stories with lists of happenings," explains Lynice. "But at six to seven they want stories with feelings, of joy and sorrow and the good and evil of fairy tales. Suddenly these mean something. This is the breathing of the soul. As we breathe in and out the soul breathes in and out through joy and sorrow. It is important to indicate this to the child for his future life."

To educate the breathing of the child in all aspects is the

essence of the Waldorf system of education. The child then becomes a person within the rhythms of life, not fixed and rigid without natural flows of in and out. At this time, too, the teachers use rhythms in speech, music and movement, linking breathing and heartbeat. The rhythm is one breath to four heartbeats in an adult, and one to five in children. This is how all Greek myths and poetic metre were formed; they are based on the relationship between breathing and heartbeat in man.

In working with rhythms at this age, they also like to give rhythm to the day. A certain time every day or week to do something, and rhythm within a lesson. There will be a time for doing something artistic and a time to do something in the feeling realm. Time spent sitting down to listen and observe and time for doing. This, says Lynice, brings the elements of feeling, thinking and willing into one lesson, so the whole child is educated all the time. "Working in the realm of feeling, everything at this stage, whether reading, writing, geography or sums is brought to the children in an artistic way. You can present things precisely but instead of being caught in abstract theory and formulae you can teach the beauty and wonder of things so they appreciate the world they are in." The children have one class teacher who stays with them from the age of seven to fourteen, so that the teacher can know the children thoroughly as individuals and see what aspects are developing. This cannot be done if teachers change for every lesson. It isn't until roughly the age of fourteen that the child becomes interested in the world of ideas and wants to unfold. He is now independent in thinking and will continue to develop and do more abstract, intellectual things, until he is twenty-one.

Steiner opened the first Waldorf School in Stuttgart in 1919, some time after he had given lectures to workers at the Waldorf Astoria cigarette factory. The lectures had been overwhelmingly successful, but the workers were more concerned for their children. The factory's managing director, Herr Emil Molt eventually agreed to finance a school for the workers' children. Steiner drew together a group of teachers, chosen for their qualities, and not necessarily people who had taught before. The schools spread, but through necessity they became fee-paying schools. Most governments will either not grant state aid to such projects or demand unacceptable controls. Therefore the schools have so far tended to become exclusively for the fairly well-off. But this is a contradiction since Steiner always emphasised his social principles. Social reform, he said, must balance the individual against his society, and as the spiritual reality of man was three-fold, in thinking, feeling and willing, this must also happen in the social body of the earth. He did not offer a political system but a clarification of elements already in existence which would help to structure and reorder things and balance life again. Any system, he said, always detracts from the vigorous life of a human being and we have got to the point where in our muddled procedures we are trying to impose standards on one another. The most vital ingredient towards the spiritual side of life is awareness.

People had come to a three-fold understanding before. The French Revolution called for Equality, Liberty and Fraternity, but it became a bloodbath because it did not have the right understanding. Equality, said Steiner, comes in the cultural life of man, and this must come before anything else. It must mean freedom for man in his mental life and concern the structure of the spiritual, creative life of each individual. This is the sphere in which we meet one another. Equality belongs to the political life, and to justice and law. Fraternity belongs to economics on which the rest of culture depends. Economics is all people in relation to all other people, said Steiner, and money, capital and goods must be on the side of brotherhood with people working together to set their own standards. We must work towards a social life in which the individual does not exploit society and the community does not suppress individuals. In this way organisations cannot be hierarchical but centrifugal, flowing from the periphery to the centre and the centre to the periphery.

To work in any state system these three principles, although working together, must be in separate spheres. The economic sphere must not interfere with the cultural (which includes education), and the rights sphere must not interfere with the economic or cultural spheres. Thus everyone has the right to have money for the work he does, but everyone has the right to the cultural life – including education – and it should not depend on the amount of money earned. Everyone, therefore, should be free to have the education he wishes. In accordance with this, a few years ago a woman called Gerry Hayn had the impulse to start with others a Waldorf School for any child whose parents wished it, regardless of the money available. The Bristol Waldorf School is a non-fee-paying school, nor does it receive support from the state. Working in the sphere of brotherhood, the parents contribute what they can afford and the teachers don't draw a fixed salary. They take what they need from a common pool when they need it, which means they can't accumulate money as they could if they were being paid wages. It seems the system consciously brings out the best in people and there is enthusiastic parental involvement. It is very much a community school.

When Lynice first arrived almost two years ago, the parents readily came along to help her paint the classroom. Originally it was blue, but because Steiner said that red is the best colour for children at this early age, they painted it red. "And I can see now that a child of six years old *is* red. The quality of red is really outward, it stands forward strong and clear. And this is what the children are, they really respond to it." The classrooms in a Waldorf School are painted to correspond to the soul mood of the children at their particular stage of development and the colours change as the children grow. Lynice has also sanded the walls so the colour moves in different shadows and isn't static. Inner movement is important for the children because everything in the world today tends towards a hardening, four-square practicality. "It is very important for their whole soul life to be fluid at this early age because this affects their thinking later on," she says. "It makes them freer, more creative." All the rooms are organised artistically and care is taken over shape. "We try not to give them too much squareness, but to show them things with curves and to have toys of wood not plastic; anything which can carry beauty in it. At this age the child observes everything and takes it all into himself. Everything you are yourself influences the children and one should be conscious of that as a teacher."

Freedom at the Waldorf School does not mean living without authority. From the age of nought to six, a child is living in the Garden of Eden in which his parents are his Gods. He has a script of dos and don'ts. From the age of seven, he begins to establish a firmer grip on the physical world. His gods become also the people outside. A child of seven wants authority, says Lynice. He believes in adults. When he gets to nine crises and changes begin to make him question things. Until that time an adult is and knows everything and, provided the adult doesn't abuse this, he is the authority to that child. It must be a natural authority, not an imposed authority. If an adult doesn't give the child that, he cannot give the child to himself.

The whole Steiner system of education is regarded as an art; the art of education. A very important aspect is art work and colour. In art, he said, we should listen to the colours first of all. A picture should come from the colours. "When we were taught art at Emerson College, they wouldn't let us paint, which was painful. We had to put colours down first and see what wanted to come out of them. It was very difficult, but also very wonderful; things can happen." Goethe did a lot of work on the quality of colours and Steiner developed this further, showing how each colour has its own objective quality to which we can penetrate if we leave our own subjective self behind. Through stories, says Lynice, she can teach the young children this. "They know how yellow rays out like the sun, how red goes forward and imposes itself and how blue holds the quality of inwardness. I might tell them about colour fairies talking to each other and making green, purple and orange. They love it that colours want to do certain things, that yellow wants to ray outwards and that if it were to go inward this would make it unhappy. If St. Michael is fighting the dragon the child could paint red, for example, and then the image of Michael comes out of the colour, expressing the action. All this corresponds to the feeling life of the child."

Steiner said young children should not be told to copy objects because it makes them rigid. This doesn't mean they mustn't draw pictures because they will, but what they draw will be an expression of something that is happening inside them. You can see this in the way very young children draw people with arms sticking out of their heads, and later, when they grow more incarnated in their body, the arms will be drawn further down. Form drawing or pattern drawing is the rhythmic repetition, as in a regular wave form, during which the emphasis is laid upon the rhythms of the movement and the inner feeling for the form. More important than external perfection is the inner movement within the child which takes place during the drawing.

Normally if people look at a Greek temple and see an acanthus leaf, they will say that the Greeks copied an acanthus leaf. Steiner said this is not true. The Greeks perceived this form inside themselves and only later realised that what man perceived inwardly was often found in the world outside. It is important that children have an inner feeling for form before they copy the outer world. In doing this they have freedom in themselves, a mind of their own. Form drawing can take many guises and changes as the children grow. Later the children will do metamorphosis of forms. This produces inner activity which affects the future thinking forces of the child; the flexibility within the form later becomes flexibility in thinking.

Another important aspect in Steiner education is in the telling of stories. He gave precise indication of the sort of stories one should tell to children and how they related to their growth. In class one, at the age of six, the children respond to fairy tales because this is where they are in their own lives. Fairy tales give a picture of the spiritual world and of the journey of the soul through the earth. "If you tell them these stories with that consciousness you are educating the children for life ahead," says Lynice. In class two the teacher begins to tell animal stories, which correspond to the stage during which the children are coming slowly from the spiritual world into earth life. "In class one, black and white, good and evil are very pure spiritual forces, but as they slowly

113

start to descend they begin to perceive the more human elements in which animals represent the exaggerated aspects of the human being. The duality in human beings is made alive by stories of animals and as a counterpart, stories of saints and holy people." Class three brings in stories of the Old Testament, a picture of a powerful father God with absolute authority and of great initiates like Moses. This also corresponds to what the children are going through, when at around the age of nine they begin for the first time to realise their separateness in the world. Where before they felt whole and held in, they now begin to question. It helps them to feel there is a strong hand over them which guides and commands them. "This sounds horrific to our modern consciousness," says Lynice, "but this is the stage the child is at. He longs for strength and authority although outwardly he questions this. Through this picture of how a child grows, we can see how humanity has grown through the ages."

By class four the stories have changed to Scandinavian myths, or Norsemen who used their will forces. Warriors who did not think but did, and who battled their way through the world, which is something the children respond to at this time. The following year is a packed one with the mythologies of the Egyptians, Persians and Greeks, an illustration of the progression of man's consciousness, coming closer now to our own age. As a child incarnates, coming slowly down to earth, these stories correspond, but at each stage the teacher is alert to the need to change. By class six, they have arrived at stories of the Romans. The Greeks were conscious of spiritual beings and personified their Gods. The Romans on the other hand were cut off from the spiritual world and became virtually the first materialists. From then on it is really teaching history, and later a teacher will introduce biographies to illustrate what ideals have driven men forward in the past.

Within the stories is a complete moral and spiritual education, a guiding of the child from the spiritual world into earthly life in a way harmonious with and corresponding to his inner development.

Astrology

"Here, now, we forget each other and ourselves.
We feel the obscurity of an order, a whole,
A knowledge, that which arranged the rendezvous,
Within its vital boundary, in the mind."

Wallace Stevens

Cosmically, something odd happened in the mid-sixties and the influence swept throughout the world. Predictably, it was felt first in America. From the moment President Kennedy was shot in 1963, all hell seemed to break loose. Standards and values had been crumbling before this, but finally they fell apart. Identification with the social system completely broke down and with the involvement in the Vietnam war, everything went haywire. People had begun to question the role of the country and society.

In astrological terms, there was a very powerful configuration around the 1960s, with Uranus conjuncting to Pluto, and Virgo opposite Saturn and Pisces. Uranus moved into Virgo in August 1962, and Pluto had already been there for some time – the rumbling of something strange had started as early as 1958-59. When Uranus began entering Virgo properly, Pluto and Uranus ran back and forth in conjunction with each other for the next few years, from 1962-68. Uranus finally left Virgo to enter Libra in 1968, although it did return for a while in June 1969. This Pluto-Uranus conjunct only happens about every 250 years and it was this that blew the old Virgo values sky high. Consciousness seemed catapulted on to another level, and identification with Virgo, which symbolises what is known and can be analysed, blew apart. All stability fell away. It was the tail end of an era and we all felt it. This was the ending of the Age of Pisces, which signified the end of everything to do with the acceptance of social values and, through its opposite, the Virgo qualities of order and pattern and structure. The teenagers of this era, now in their early thirties, unconsciously sensed they were in at the beginning of a new thing. It was the dawning of the Age of Aquarius.

The Beatles personified it all. When an archetype or a particular value or aspect of a new value is trying to emerge from the unconscious on a collective level, it needs new areas of experience to develop in. Consequently it appears first of all as a fad and there is great attachment to it on an emotional level. For example, we might buy a copy of *Vogue* because it describes a fashion which is in our consciousness. If, as over the last few years, it shows Arabic influence, this is saying something that is happening between two cultures. When the Beatles approached the Maharishi, half the world began meditating because they were emotionally attracted to the fad; people became attached to the glamour. The whole hippy movement was an unconscious emotional reaction to a new emerging value. Like children, the only way to understand it was through the glamour. They became hooked on 'getting into consciousness' by taking LSD and screaming and shouting and experiencing each other. Underneath the fad there was a very deep need. The New Age was trying to come in, but the hippies and freaks couldn't carry it through because they were confused and insecure within themselves. This does not negate the basic quality of love and anti-war they were trying to initiate. They were really trying to change the world.

The universal law is that for any new energy to come into consciousness, whether in an individual or in the form of a collective New Age for mankind, it must come first in a crude germ form and gradually refine. When the new energy of love and peace came in, it needed a period of development. Refinement necessarily means distortion which is part of the evolutionary process of growth. On a personal level, if a new energy like love is coming through for us, it tends at first to run riot, and we find ourselves throwing ourselves on people, so anxious are we to love them. But we have to go through this process in order for it to become clear and refined. That is what was happening during this era. There were some magnificent barbarians plunging 'into group consciousness'. But once you strip away all the glamour the bare bones begin to show and the real need begins to emerge.

Because it is not spherical, the earth wobbles as it orbits around the sun on its polar axis. Because the polar axis is fixed and always points the same way, due north shifts in relation to the rest of the universe. Each year therefore when the sun enters Aries, the backdrop of stars behind have moved slightly. Every 2000 years we get a completely different constellation and the whole circle through the twelve ortho-dox constellations takes roughly 26,000 years to complete. There seems to be a striking relationship between the constellation of the vernal equinox and the collective ar-chetype in the unconscious.

It appears that archetypes come up from the collective unconscious each 2000 years and correspond to the change in the constellation, and like the psyche of each individual, the collective value of each astrological age refines and develops over the 2000 years. We see this most effectively in religious symbolism. The astrological sign ruling an age does not say how human beings will behave, but how they will project their God image. In 4,000 BC the Age of Taurus began. The tribes which were previously hunters and nomads began to settle and till the earth. This was the start of the agricultural society, the Tigris Euphrates era in Egypt, when man finally became related to the earth. The Taurean Age brought with it the cult of the Mother Goddess, and all the religious symbolism reflected earth and the process of development. God was in the demonic forces to which man prayed in awe. Man was nothing.

In the Age of Aries, which began in 2000 BC the matriarchy

ended and it became the age of the hero. The power of man's will. Mother was no longer supreme because there was a father in the sky. God moved closer to the human being in that with the demi-gods of the Greeks man could argue and communicate with his God.

At the time of Christ the dawning of the new era brought a new God value in connection with Pisces. It was in the Piscean Age that all religions: Islam, Buddhism, Christianity required the submission of the individual. They were feeling-oriented religions. God meant worship and was manifest in daily life. Craftsmen like those of the Renaissance painted and sculpted for the glory of God. Coming still closer to man, God incarnated as a man, he became human just once. For 1500 years the Piscean value was in the belief in the science of superstition. Everything was a miracle. Spirit as the alchemists said was the same as matter. But over the last 500 years it began to veer off-course. Its opposite Virgo value, the other polar extreme produced a reversal of values. With the age of enlightenment has come the growing belief that nothing is real except matter, that God does not exist.

At the beginning of each New Age, new gods are born and the structure of society goes through a massive transformation. This is happening right now. The collective psyche is going through a death and rebirth. Old laws of energy are losing their potency and new laws are being introduced. This started at the beginning of the last century and will continue over roughly a hundred years. The crossover point will probably occur at the end of this century, and there are some odd conjunctions lining up towards the end of the century which will inevitably bring metaphorical tidal waves and earthquakes.

The Aquarian Age still concerns science but in a less materialistic sense. It is to do with knowledge. Science will take away the mysteries that once made it necessary to project on to an outer God. Men will tame the powers of nature and make them available to man. God has been approaching man for 6000 years and now, in this Age, God will be in man. God will be in everyone, and it is this we begin to realise in consciousness as we sense the link with Self and the higher values of the universe. It is a knowledge that successive generations will have quite automatically as the age continues to refine and develop.

That this conscious knowledge has been emerging on a wide scale only over the last few years also has astrological significance. Pluto moved into Leo just before the outbreak of the last war and people born with Pluto in Leo seem most susceptible to these things. Pluto has very deep roots in collective changes, in the source of all things underground and of everything that comes from it. This heralded the beginning of the generation which could not accept anything which did not come out of Self. Pluto moved into Leo in September 1938, for the first time for 250 years and finally left in 1957. There was therefore a twenty year span of people born with Pluto in Leo, a whole generation who could no longer accept outward values and consequently everything began to break loose.

Of course this consciousness has come to people of all ages, but since it has only been emerging widely over the last six or so years, it follows that the link with Self has been triggered most naturally during the traumatic Saturn return cycle of people within the twenty-eight to thirty-one age group. When this happens there is a concerted thrust from the unconscious to liberate the developing personality from the pull of the past and launch it on to a quest into the future. It would seem then, that those with the greater sense of this at the moment are people now in their late twenties and thirties.

Astrology, explains Liz, is a map of the energies which motivate life, the basic laws by which life operates. It is the analysis of the expression of certain patterns and if you want to call them Jupiter, Mars and Saturn, that is fine, it provides nice imagery. If you want to call them Shiva and Brahmin in the language of Eastern mysticism, or quarks and sub-atomic particles in the language of Quantum Physics, these are equally rich vocabularies also concerned with the plan by which life unfolds itself. Astrology is the language of religion. A manifestation of the unmanifest in time. With the decline of old religious guidance, man needs guidance within his own psyche, not from outside. No human being can really see the whole pattern but the more man works with some of these symbols, the more he can begin to grasp it. "The more you amplify your vocabulary to use other systems," says Liz, "the more insight you may have. Myths, fairy tales and quantum physics, they are all intuitively talking about the same things, as anything is, which attempts to understand the laws by which life operates and to discover its meaning and purpose."

Once she had discovered astrology, Liz studied it with passion. She began to do charts professionally while still at college. Once you know the steps, she says, provided you have the right books and tables to calculate a chart, it involves only simple mathematics. "Everyone must begin in the same place by memorising planets and what they mean in each sign. If you have Gemini rising it means you are communicative, chatty and interested in idea. The person then says you are crazy or yes, that's me, and if he says you're crazy you have to make out why. It was by having dialogues with person after person that I began to get my own interpretations. A lot is intuition."

With a Ph.D she became both Astrologer and Counsellor, but everything changed for her when she was introduced to Jungian psychology. "A light came on and then everything made sense," she says. "It was a psychology that finally spoke to me, as opposed to the kind I had been taught. After that it clicked that astrology and psychology were just different vocabularies." Jung's map of the psyche, as much as he was able to complete in his lifetime, described not only the structure of the individual psyche with conscious and unoconscious, and the four functions of thinking, feeling, sensation and intuition, but also the collective unconscious. The collective unconscious is what the esoterics call 'group soul', the entire field for life, including the solar system. Jung carefully said we don't know what it is, only that is has no limits. What he presented was an empirical map, which is the same thing that esoterics offer in their description of the solar system, a living being with complex energy centres in that living being. "Everything he described seemed borne out by astrological symbolism and everything he had come across working with people in psychology fitted the same map, they were just different words. Not in an absolutely literal way, but so close tht he could have invented astrology."

Few good astrologers would claim that the same transit involving the same planets, yet affecting two different individuals, will produce exactly the same effects, says Liz. Not only are the individual's charts different, but you must also consider the environment, the current circumstances, the sex, the particular psychic constitution and the present level of awareness of each. All that can be said is that the inner meaning of the transit is the same. "As soon as we begin talking about the meaning of an event to the individual," says Liz, "we are no longer dealing with external circumstances but with the psyche. We find ourselves in the domain of analytical psychology, which attempts to explore the laws governing and regulating the psyche's activities. It is in the study of planetary transits and progressions and what they indicate of the individual's development that astrology and psychology have most to offer each other. Psychology can provide astrology with a framework that makes its symbols comprehensible and relevant in human terms. At the same time astrology can offer psychology a blueprint of the individual's potential, which not only determines what kind of seed, but what timing and what patterns of growth must be considered."

Life is eternally in motion and so are human beings. The birthchart indicates what a person's potential could be and the progressions of the horoscope are a symbolic way of showing the inner timing of psychic events; they show what areas of that potential are being highlighted at different periods in life to give the opportunity for conscious recognition and integration.

The significance of astrology lies not in our physical chunk of rock orbiting the sun but in the quality of a moment in time. It is the same principle as that of *I Ching*, the Chinese Book of Changes. In *I Ching* the questions and the moment react on each other, and as the conscious reflects the moment, so the hexagram reflects the question. If you freeze the moment in time, the quality of life at that moment will have certain attributes and everything in life will reflect what those attributes are. Everything is a moment of energy and if you freeze it, that pattern of energy will visibly show in many different ways. "Australian aborigines could get it from the formation of the clouds," says Liz, "the Chinese by throwing coins. There is a basic individual quality to a moment and the planets are one of many things which can be used as indicators of those qualities. By reading a chart you do not make anyone do anything. All people are part of the same pattern, so you synchronistically correspond."

Every civilisation used its own astrological references, but many differ in their interpretations. Interpretation grows partly from a tradition of thousands of years of observation. Patterns repeat themselves in nature and can be chosen as archetypal symbols representing a tree, a rock or the entire galaxy. Interpretations differ also for cultural reasons, but in the final analysis, none of these differences really matter, because most of astrological interpretation is a matter of intuition.

An astrological chart, however it is produced, gives no more than an inkling of what the personality could be; of personal potential. "I have never met anyone who has lived his whole chart," Liz says. "Certainly not until very old and still things remain untapped. The object is to become oneself and any consultation comes down to that. How much on the map is conscious and how much is not being used; how much are you clinging to one part and how much fighting with another. Discovering oneself is what all these systems are about. They are there to make you more or less conscious."

You consult a horoscope to find out what your psyche is up to because you have so little awareness of the matrix of life from which the conscious ego springs. The chart is a map of your intuition. Some intuitive people have great sensitivity to inner timing that regulates endings and beginnings of phases, a knack for divining the moving forces of the unconscious. The chart is a confirmation of that intuition. Ideally we should not need anything, we are each our own living map, except that in the West we have come so far from our understanding of this, it is impossible to maintain the connection. The problem lies in becoming crystalised and thinking the map is the world. "I reached the point where astrology went stale on its own," says Liz. "I had to amplify it with psychology, mythology, comparative religion, dream analysis, anything I could get my hands on in the way of maps. If you stare at a map too long you begin to get hung up on it. You read a map if you want to travel from A to B, but if you are looking at the map all the time you forget the scenery. Only if you get badly lost do you need to go back to the map."

Psychology

*"In the self-consciousness of man, Life
has gone to its limits. To go further,
self-consciousness must be transcended
and that can only be done by way of the
self and of that consciousness."*

Michael Adam

From the moment she met Roberto Assagioli in October
1974, Diana knew that Psychosynthesis was her life's work.
Assagioli knew it too. She spent a week with him this first
time and he cancelled appointments with other students so
they could meet twice a day. At the end of this week she was
desperate to study properly with him and, with the assistance
of a little synchronicity, she did. Roberto had been ill and
couldn't take students. No one was with him except his
co-workers, but among them was Pierro Furruci, who was
going away for the summer. Pierro, who now works with
Diana, encouraged her to ask Roberto if she could replace
him. This she did in June 1975.

Diana was with Assagioli during the three months before
he died. "Afterwards I saw clearly that I didn't go to study
with Roberto, but to serve him and be with him at the end of
his life." she says. "Unconsciously I was going not for me but
for him." The Italians around him put him on a pedestal. He
was a lonely man because no one met him eye to eye as a

human being. Assagioli adored Diana and she him. Usually students saw him twice a week, but she was with him for six hours a day. She worked for him, typing letters and editing papers for the book he was writing, and an hour a day was for her. Since he had no formal training programme, he taught her Psychosynthesis by giving her therapy. She was with him for the forty-eight hours before he died. "Watching his body die was very frightening," she says. "But on another level he looked forward to death, he saw it as a liberation. For his soul it was a very positive thing. I was horrified and delighted at the same time."

From Italy Diana went straight on to work with a core of eight people at the Psychosynthesis Institute in California. Here she began her study, seriously working at the same time, and after a year she joined the London Institute. Today she works for herself. "I find now that I can be more creative with Psychosynthesis when I don't have anyone controlling me," she says. "Assagioli's teaching said that anything which promotes wholeness is acceptable, he had no dogma, and all institutions have a tendency to become rigid and confined in structures." By leaving the Institute she was able to expand towards her own sense of freedom.

Psychosynthesis, which sees the personality as the vehicle for expression of the spiritual self, says that therapy cannot do anything *to* you. This is a totally different attitude to most psychology which says 'become my client and I will make you better. Take this magic pill and all will be well'. This attitude can do more harm than good, says Diana, because the client doesn't learn to take care of and nourish himself. Instead he can become dependent on the guide, teacher or therapist. The emphasis in psychosynthesis is that the individual has his own power, and everything he needs to find his own way. This means he takes an active part and accepts responsibility for his own existence. The 'guide' cannot know what is right for you. This is the purpose of your life. What the guide does is help you find that path, the direction of your life and then helps you deal with any obstacles to that. It is like a parent watching a child learning to walk. Too many parents run in and catch the child in case he falls and hinder his ability to learn. A good parent has to let him fall. Pain is not a negative thing, it is part of life.

Naturally growth is best done spontaneously but you can 'become aware' through techniques. The people who come to Diana for guidance are mostly what she calls 'healthy neurotics'. People who have everything they need on the material level and are fairly successful in whatever they do, but find there is something missing. Psychosynthesis is concerned with the existential crisis of meaning. People from all walks of life who think, here I am, I have accomplished what I set out to do, and I'm still not happy. What is the meaning of it all? During the last few years she has been focusing her guidance on professionals, on group leaders and therapists. She personally believes that people working with people should be constantly reassessing themselves.

One of the main objectives of Psychosynthesis is to show that each of us is a whole and total organism, and that we should be expanding our consciousness to see in a holistic way. We tend only to think of our body or our feelings and forget we have other parts to our personality. We also tend to think that we are what is wrong with us, that we are our negative aspects. Psychosynthesis says, yes we are these, but we are also our positive ones. Psychosynthesis says, yes this is what is wrong, now what is right? The subpersonalities, the semi-autonomous figures in our unconscious imposed on us by our backgrounds and lifestyles, do have this negativity but we must discover the things they have which are positive.

Psychosynthesis says we want wholeness not perfection. It changes the perspective in which we see ourselves. It begins by saying that our essence, our essential Self is pure beingness. Our Self has a totally subjective rightness, and once we eliminate the blocks in our personality we can begin to experience what is right for us and be true to that Self. What is wrong with us takes away from who we really are. We may think we are rising above our jealousy or anger of selfishness, but often we are just sitting on them. As we begin to contact this direct sense of Self, certain energies leap from it, like the sun sending its energies into the world. The closer we are to experiencing ourselves as an energy of transpersonal qualities, the more in touch we are with ourselves. The major theory in Psychosynthesis deals with Purpose, Intention and Plan. Purpose is the Transpersonal Will or Self, and in any problem we are looking at the 'Higher Self's' purpose. When the 'personal' comes in to Diana for therapy with its intention and she tries to look at the intention of the personal will, theoretically she is trying to align the one with the other. Psychosynthesis finds the purpose of the 'Higher Self' and tries to connect with that and therefore with the purpose of a person's life.

During an introductory two-day workshop which Diana asks all her clients to do, a group of up to sixteen people will work through the various aspects of Psychosynthesis from the purely psychological to the idea of the transpersonal or higher self. To work with the unconscious elements Psychosynthesis uses images rather than words. Images are the language of the unconscious, both the 'lower' and the 'higher', because the unconscious does not use words. Images are better to work with because they are symbolic. Jung worked a great deal with dream images, which change dramatically when the psyche is in a state of transition and needs to be heard. Images are powerful transformers of psychic energy.

She will use various exercises and techniques, such as the guided daydream, which requires the group simply to let their mind wander in whatever way it chooses, as she talks them through the sequence. Sometimes, particularly at the beginning, imaging may seem difficult. Either images don't want to come, or they seem to be consciously conjured up through the intellect as it thinks necessary. But, as Diana points out, the fact that our conscious mind has chosen that particular image is also meaningful, and this 'excuse' is not really valid. Even if we think of an image we already know, the fact that we chose it at that moment is significant. Understanding this, all you need do is relax and enjoy the exercise.

The guided daydream is a technique used to bring to the surface aspects of ourselves which we would not normally allow to come to us in consciousness. The exercise brings new insights to ground you more deeply into yourself, as well as to clarify and introduce the idea of a deeper meaning and purpose to whatever you are doing. The real workshop is life of course, but Psychosynthesis can be valuable to the life process in finding out where you are in your life right now, what the direction of your life is and where you need to put more energy. It is a way of looking inward without any strain. The exercises are done sitting comfortably or lying down. A first exercise, which may take up to forty minutes, is to discover the subpersonalities, the figures in our unconcious that may be in conflict. Everyone in the group lies down in a comfortable position on the floor, closing their eyes and 'relaxing down'. Diana then asks the group to imagine themselves in a meadow. At the end of this meadow is a house which they enter, and once they are quite familiar with the house they come back outside and sit down a little way beyond it. She then tells them to imagine three or four people coming out of the house to talk with them and to each other, to find out who they are and what they want. Once the conversation is over, the people return to the house and the door is closed. The house represents the psyche, your own inner space, and the people inside are your subpersonalities. Symbolically you are opening the door on to a different level of consciousness.

Our negative behaviour is merely a particular subpersonality making a noise, asking us to hear it. It is saying that some part of us needs something. If we listen and tune in and accept the negative behaviour it will dissipate. We name the people in order to make a relationship with them. Diana, for example, says that she originally found a 'frightened child' subpersonality and wanted to get rid of her. "When I worked with her I found she was six years old and needed love." She also had an 'angry person' who wanted to punch people on the nose and a 'learner' person, who didn't know anything but just had to be in the position of the learner.

As with all the models of the psyche used, for some people this exercise is very appropriate, for others it is not, but if significant material does come up and you want to know what it says, you can look at it in terms of real life. There are certain core figures and some that turn up once and you never see again. It is a here and now statement about your lifestyle. In a month's time when your life has moved on, things will have changed.

The exercise continues. Diana asks everyone to walk around the room acting out one of the subpersonalities, reacting to the other people in the room on that level. She then makes you be the opposite of that subpersonality and act out the feelings of whatever that opposite might be. Finally, standing on the floor, you take up a stance that represents this feeling and make a representative movement, first for the subpersonality and then for its opposite. Thus you are choosing to identify with one part of yourself and then with its opposite, which is also within you. Moving back and forth between the two gives them energy and by acknowledging the two sides they can come together more harmoniously. If we identify with one extreme there is always a pull from the opposite. This identification by its nature causes the opposite pole to start screaming. In her private work, if someone is identifying with the one, Diana tries to energise the opposite. They will never reach that opposite, but this moves them towards the centre.

The aim of these exercises is to understand that it is not our totality which is immature, but only part of us. There is a place inside us, part of our personality, which can move and make choices and can identify with this one part if it chooses. If we do choose to identify unconsciously with this part, we can lose ourselves in it. But it is possible to step back in consciousness out of this role, into a centre of pure consciousness that knows the problem and the solution. A centre which gives us freedom of choice and allows us to take responsibility for our own actions. This centre in our personality is the first part to communicate with the centre of the 'Higher Self', it is a mirror reflection of that Self, and once you have a sense of this centre you are moving very much closer to the Self. Although we cannot live in the Self all the time, at any one moment we can step into our centre and have closer contact with that 'I'.

The process of 'disidentification' from the subpersonalities helps to recognise them, own them and accept them. The next step is to try and find out their needs and then to step back. You may recognise the 'good girl', but this is not who you are. We can say I have a mind, but I am not my mind. I have emotions, but I am not my emotions. I have a body, but I am not my body. This is part of the process of becoming centred, and with the guided daydream technique it leads to the development of skill in stepping back into the centre. Like a muscle, the more you use it, the stronger it gets.

Any 'disidentification' exercise is a Will exercise, says Diana, because it is part of the unfoldment towards the real 'I'. The goal in Psychosynthesis is not to solve the problems but to become our own master in a self-regulating way, rather than be the victim of our drives, instincts and emotions. Anything which goes towards this, is developing the Will, helping you to become the conductor of an orchestra instead of a collection of independent instruments. Once the personality becomes more solid, Psychosynthesis then emphasises the higher, spiritual Self and endeavours to build a communication between the two.

Of course the transpersonal energy is always present. There is something inside us, a source of wisdom, an inner guide, that knows who we are and where we are going. A part that knows what we need to do and how we can do it. In 'psychosynthesis' terms, it is the 'Higher Self' which knocks on the door and energises those parts of the personality that can get us going in the right direction. By giving her 'frightened child' love, Diana says, she eventually got to what this part had to give, which is sensitivity. If she pushed her away she lost that sensitivity. When her 'learner' subpersonality controlled her, she had nothing to contribute, but when she got in touch with her learner, she discovered that its strengths lay in curiosity and an excitement about life. If a subpersonality is aggressive, this is often pushed away. The core of this might be a strength but it has become distorted to aggression. Each subpersonality ultimately has some superconscious quality to express for the Self. Their 'negative' behaviour is really only a distortion of their essential nature and quality. We must find the thing which the subpersonality is seeking to express, some quality that is trying to bring to our lives. The 'Higher Self' will move to make it available.

The Transpersonal is the part connected with the intuition and during the workshop Diana instigates various ways in which we may become aware of the link between this and the conscious mind. One form is in free drawing, which is an ideal way to see what is going on in the psyche. To sit and let the hand do and see what comes out, looking rather than interpreting. A second way is through a guided daydream about climbing a mountain. At the top you are told to meet a wise person who tells you what is stopping you from doing what you want to do. Symbolically the wise person is you, not something outside you. It is a way of tickling the intuition and opening yourself to it. It is a way of promoting trust in something inside you which can tell you what you have to do. It establishes the idea that intuition is a real and valid part of you.

As she becomes more synthesised herself, Diana is beginning more easily to sense the soul or 'Higher Self' in her clients and sense how this Self is trying to guide them. "If a client is coming to me with an emotional problem, I think what is the higher Self trying to do in energising that problem and now I clearly have a sense of what that is. If I meditate on a client before a session and on what needs to happen, I'll get an answer which nine times out of ten is right. It frightens me, it's so right.

"My work is soul infusion and deals with the living spirit in my clients, and my sensitivity is beginning to have a strong sense of each person. Sometimes when I'm working with a person, if they are having trouble or resisting something or are stuck, I just look or talk inwardly to their higher Self and ask it to give this person that little thing they need and again, nine times out of ten, it works. It is almost like magic to me. It is in my work that I contact my own soul most."

Art

"But whereas in all else there is effortlessness,
in the willow and the wild deer, man is still a
creature of strain. Understandably, for man
has a new step to learn, a new leap to take, and
it is only likely that he will stumble if he is
to venture out of the old sure ways, if he is
ever to overrun the careful confines of himself."

Michael Adam

Although the head of the Royal College of Art was interested in her work, Lorraine did not apply. She felt that art was about living and experience. An artist is a channel for the experience of life, which comes through him as a form of truth. The only difference between life and art is the language, which in art is the language of colour and line on a flat surface. If a student spends years in college, what is he going to channel?

When at twenty-nine, after the revelation, she rejected the traditional teaching of art, she felt that she had reached a stage of no return, a point of stability from which to move on. "I didn't know where I was going, but I knew I had found the nucleus, the subject matter that I had been looking for to express my being." In its affirmation of her position on the planet, the revelation gave her a sense of belonging to past, present and future. She didn't consider life and death separately because death was as much a part of her as life. This feeling anchored her emotions, she says, and enabled her to sit down and paint out of that experience.

She began to draw from somewhere she didn't know and made the rough for a painting in three parts, a painting which indicated what she felt about the past, present and future of man. It just flowed out of her pencils and she knew she had left another stage of herself behind. She became a work machine, her commitment was absolute. She knew she could not waver in her mission. She felt a tremendous power of the will to manifest her entire being through her work as long as she lived.

In the painting of the past, the canvas is divided by two diagonal lines of red and yellow, which symbolise light cutting through. Man is shown in symbolic white, half submerged in a bacterial sea of change. The second canvas has circular forms, although not quite reaching the full circle. A diagonal of light still shines through, but man is totally submerged in the sea of change. The sea looks violent with waves like the fins of sharks. There is a touch of light on man and a closed flower beginning to open its bud to the light.

What she experienced from the revelation of the oak tree was a sense of colour and light; the flowing of life in everything that could be seen. "Life was such a miracle of heightened awareness and beauty, it felt impossible for me to do damage to anything. The only way to express that in painting was to try to find colour and light that would energise and change and be beautiful in a transient way, in the way that line really was." Her sense of reality told her not to be afraid of transience. This was the process of change, as the vibration of the glow of life fell and rose again, each stage fluctuating from one to the other. This she knew was the greatness that was life. Life was not stable or absolute, and one line could not make do for an image. The image should be transient and changing, taking on different forms because this is how we see. People are changing all the time, and beauty is accepting change. We should not hope that things will stand still for our security. "This is why my language became abstract, because it was impossible to depict an image of change and beauty with an absolute image which told only one story. That one story was only taking one element out of life. Abstract and colour and light encompassed all things. Change came by a metamorphosis into different shapes."

In the painting of the future she felt she had to express a new way of making an angle which would convey man as he would become in terms of the consciousness she had just felt. The third painting was blue with a diagonal cutting through. The form had then become a circle. A three-pointed spear was floating away in space, within the circle representing the microcosm and the macrocosm. "The circle was this element of colour reaching its new forms of light in consciousness. In one tiny little area of that painting I made one white cross, a religious symbol, but a cross also represents a vertical and horizontal which are two stable elements and all the colour which came from that cross was the reincarnation and eternal life which colour and light give. Cézanne made us aware of our changing perceptions by the fact that he broke up space into little coloured units and didn't make one solid outline in any painting. I realised then what his endeavour and terrible struggle had been. At that point too I fully realised my position as a painter, my responsibility and the love and gratitude for all the painters who have been before me. I also realised how very little is known about the art of making an image."

From the third painting she discovered that she was talking about energy and light as created by colour in the mind of the beholder. She realised this was the struggle underlying the evolution of painting and the very structure that underlies matter by which we direct our environment. Through the experience of being at one with the process of pounding energy, she had realised that this was a process of light. "If we look at something we can only see it because of the way light affects it. So, you ask, what is the nature of light?" She began to look more seriously at the way colour interrelated in natural phenomena. The only way we can see is by the reflection or refraction of light from matter, and from this arise the basic colours of the spectrum. Her thought continued that if you hone that down you should be able to get this by using just three colours.

The language of painting is academically difficult, but she became aware that she was in fact doing 'molecular' painting. She knew she had to find out more about the function of the planet, the relationship of all human beings and life, and to understand what we know about matter and the comprehensive essence that lies behind it. The connections seemed so important that she needed to study seriously. She studied everything that seemed relevant: quantum physics, molecular structure, Renaissance perspective, physics, geology, astrology. She was finding out what gives rise to various forms of matter, and putting this in alignment with what she felt she had discovered. During that time books and other references fell in a synchronistic way into her hands. She was making great connections between what were called 'illogical' discoveries, things that had not been connected before; Don Juan's 'lines of the world' connected to perspective in art, and also to the revelations of Jung and Teilhard de Chardin; Leonardo da Vinci's themes of light and vision connected to scientific analysis and how the visual process responds to the environment. All these things suddenly became comprehensible and complimentary to what she was trying to discover in painting.

It meant she had to go back to the sources of structure and colour and how we observe them. "I thought I would have to go back to realise the importance of painting as a perceptual mechanism, and I took the structure of painting down to a minimum of three lines and three colours. It was a great wrench after my education in art, but I felt this was correct. I felt I had to go back to the source to understand where we are now. To create any illusion of depth on a flat surface means you have to use three basic lines; a horizontal to correspond to the horizon, an oblique to give the illusion of depth and a vertical to represent all the uprights in the environment. I began to paint three random lines and three colours in complexity on canvas and, at the point where I felt that the painting was instinctively finished, I thought this is it, I must be totally crazy. Three lines, three colours, what is there in this that is going to satisfy any visual perceptions?

"But I found my perception responded by selecting its own order from these lines and I realised that the brain needs to create order out of chaos. It was a great revelation to me, because I realised painting had got to the stage where you could make optical paintings. You can give the impression of anything, from a flock of birds to a seagull, by purely optical painting, by formulating those three lines and colours. It was a struggle with the intuition. I was arriving at a synthesis between science and art. For years the representational painter has seen grass and trees in word terms. I was working out a structure of visual phenomena through observation, making similar patterns in the visual sense as our interconnecting brain does. Colour and sound were from the same source."

From that third painting came a series of thirty. She worked for eighteen months non-stop, producing them one after the other; once completing a painting in just two days. Images and visions came to her both at night and during the day, and she could hardly keep up with her own energy. She lived, ate and slept her work and has never been happier. The end of that series culminated in an enormous three-part painting which was made on the floor of her attic; a painting nine feet square, in three-foot sections. Able to look at each painting along the nine foot length, she could see the meaning of the entire composition in perspective as well as evaluate each unit independently. Each part was as full of miracles as the whole. As is each part of the whole sphere of life. A universal concept. She could begin at last to illustrate to the observer how the observer's perceptions actually functioned. How the observer was participating. In the past the painter has told us what we are seeing, but now in painting the observer could be involved, he could see his own perceptual process at work. "I thought I was crazy to take such a cold way of seeing things but now I feel I have confirmed that to involve human beings in the process of your paintings is much more human than to paint a scene so that they have to be told what to see."

Her confidence became unshakeable in that nothing people might say about her painting could alter the knowledge that things change in a good and positive way. "My work was only a manifestation of that and it was going to happen. I wasn't afraid in terms of my own ego of what would happen or what people would say." But she did want to know how people responded to what she felt was the truth in them. In 1973 she held an exhibition in Oxford, at which the paintings were not to be sold. It was an interesting moment and the reaction was ninety-per-cent positive. She felt that the truth of her painting was recognised and confirmed by the criticism of the paintings with which she herself did not feel happy.

Her paintings are to do with human potential in her terms. What she saw in the David was a very simple thing. That one small man with enough drive and willpower and dedication could create a colossal work of beauty. This knowledge told her overwhelmingly that man could do anything and everything he wanted to do, if he wanted it badly enough. "It made me see how little people did with their lives when it was possible to do so much. It made me take up the burden of my own life. It was either to do that or put it aside and live life out totally meaninglessly."

The story of course does not all run smoothly. Lorraine was virtually wiped out after her massive effort, to the point where she was given two months to live. She had exhausted her heart and at one point was given acupuncture every two hours for twenty-four hours. An important relationship ended and an exhibition organised for her while she was ill was a flop because her paintings had been far too highly priced. All this set her back two years.

The sheer mechanics of being a painter who must earn her living are terrifying. Physical endurance is unending. She hauled furniture and humped carpets to fix her attic studio alone. Fetching and carrying canvas stretchers is exhausting in itself. Her struggle to express herself on the painting level as well as on the personal level, was such that at times she says she felt insecure to the point where everything felt hopeless, that the conflicts were never going to end. She consoled herself with the thought that she was ahead of her time. "I was totally sure that there was going to be another time of Renaissance long before I heard anything to do with enlightenment and New Age consciousness. Now, when I think back, it has become rather commonplace for groups of people to be searching for enlightenment. Then, I was totally overwhelmed by the context of it, because there was no way of saying it to anyone else I knew."

To paint what she feels, she must be in constant conscious contact with the forces of life. The conflict between being a painter and a human being is a constant problem. This has always been so for artists. "Since I learned that there are very few people to talk to, I have moved into a much more balanced day to day living," she says. "In the beginning I had the incoherence of a fanatic, but my vision has seen itself through, and now I recognise that it is a lifetime job and that time has its own rhythms. I must recognise within myself how much I can do in what I am given."

In an age of technology and computers, she says, art has been left behind. Most artists do not think that art has anything to do with science and technology cannot find a way of incorporating creative abilities. She is including technology with art, bringing science and the imagination together. Art is still concerned with basic post-war pop art, there has been no major step towards a new vision. Art teachers are not really taught any art history to help them interpret the grammar of painting. Art is taught as therapy, not as a practical and basic perceptual skill.

In terms of art history the first quantum leap of consciousness was in making an image which would enhance survival. Then, during the Egyptian era, an image was made to help the victim in the religious sense against things that oppressed him. The next major advance was made by the Greeks who explored nature in a more fundamental way and aligned it with their politics and geometrical theory. Then all was quiet until the quantum leap of Renaissance when vision was formalised into three-dimensional linear perspective. This persisted for three hundred years until Cézanne, realising that perspective worked from incident to incident, anticipated Einstein by breaking up space and time and inventing artistic relativity.

"As far as I'm concerned, a painter has to look very deeply

into art history and into themselves to find out where they are in perspective," says Lorraine. "I have simplified even further all these discoveries, which means that I have gone right back to the source to make it more evident that our perceptions are based in a very practical way, not only in art but in our functioning as human beings within our environment. This is why I now work with computers because I believe that art will be incorporated into modern day technology.

"With Cézanne the art world broke up into cubism and then on to pop and op art and abstract expressionism. It turned into a many-headed monster, a salad of art and I believe out of every salad comes a new order. Now I feel we are ripe for a new order which has to be a synthesis of all these trends in terms of going back to their fundamental source and then reorganising them, and linking them with the present day, which means technology and science. I feel a woman of my time and I think it can be done more easily as a woman because I have not been sacrificed to ambition. I have had the simplicity to reach back."

Lorraine's art is visually acceptable, but not yet commercial. "There are no positive supports behind me except insofar as what I have earned. No one to hand me a gallery or articles to write, so I do not have any security around me. But at last I have recognised that it is within my power to go out and earn my security; it is what I have been doing now totally on my own. I can only grow in confirmation of my truth which came about through things inside me; things made manifest. I also know that those things are existent in all people who choose to do that and in whatever work they decide to do. Painting is a tangible expression of who I am. My painting is my peace."

Healing

*"The prerequisite of originality
is the art of forgetting for the
moment what we know. Hence the
importance of the unconscious
who puts reason to sleep and
restores for a transient moment
the innocence of vision."*

Arthur Koestler

As a nurse, there were things in western medicine that began to bother Isobel. Firstly, whenever she was ill herself the symptoms were never easily diagnosed. This raised the question of diagnosis. And secondly she began to dislike the way medicine was going in the constant administration of drugs. Methods were becoming so technical that doctors were beginning to forget their patients were human beings. In allopathic medicine the emphasis was on the diagnosis of problems, treating the symptoms and if possible removing the cause. In other words, in trying to fit the individual to the system, doctors were looking for the problems and setting things right. She was certain there must be other ways of thinking.

At the health farm at Tyringham she learned about alternative kinds of medicine, about naturopathic cures which emphasised the ideal state of health and how this could

140

be achieved. Yet these too, she felt, were looking at the situation in the wrong way. The original idea of acupuncture was that a doctor kept you well and if you became ill you stopped paying him until he made you well again. What the so-called alternative methods, like naturopathy, homeopathy and acupuncture have done is turn the idea round. Today acupuncture says, yes, this is about getting you into a state of good health; now, let's treat these symptoms. They haven't changed the thinking, only the form. Instead of using surgery they are using needles, and because the practice is Eastern, people believe this must be more natural. It is still the allopathic method under the homeopathic name. "Everyone is stuck on finding what is wrong," says Isobel, "not finding what is right. People have forgotten to switch." She feels that she has had to get to the point of perceiving rightness, because the majority of people are stuck on wrongness. We are conditioned to believe in it.

The body has an extraordinary ability to heal itself if there is nothing interfering. All of us have the ability to heal ourselves and the ability to impart some of our energies to those in need. This is what healing is about. Isobel had already had some experience of this as a young nurse. "I read a Harry Edward's book in which he said that anybody could heal. So I said, 'okay, I can heal'. I was sitting in my room, off-duty – the hospital was ten miles away – and thought of the most ill person I could, who I couldn't bring any harm to. I just thought of this young man who was very ill and had the feeling of making contact with him, directing a 'beam of energy' at him. I forgot about it, but two nights later I went back on duty and the bed was empty. The man was watching television and no one knew why but he had begun to pick up on Saturday afternoon. I did a similar thing for a cancer patient on the ward. His wife was expecting a baby and was told he wouldn't be there when the baby was born. He came to a crisis one night and again I had a feeling to do something. His high temperature dropped to normal and he did live to see the baby; he lived for about two years."

She didn't ever say anything and was frightened to heal again, because she felt either she must understand the ability to heal, or not do it at all. But healing she knew is simply being open, getting out of the way of the life energies. "Most straight medicine is interfering with the healing process," says Isobel. "Some of it is good interference, some not good. Obviously it is complex because the interference can come from the mind, body or spirit or from foreign bodies, anything. But I think a lot of people treated medically, heal themselves in spite of, and not because of, treatment. Basically, for the less serious conditions, the less you do the better. If we work to restore the balance of the system then the symptoms may disappear."

As soon as she was introduced to the Alexander Technique she knew that at last someone was speaking the right language. If you look at the overall pattern and set up the mind and body so it has the least possible interference, the right thing is simply allowed to do itself. In another context this could be called healing, but Alexander called it psychophysical re-education. Frederick Matthias Alexander was an actor in the early 1900s. Through trying to restore his own voice from having traumatically lost it, his Principle began to unfold. He became aware that because of bad use of his body, through the habits of a lifetime, he was causing the problem himself. He realised the importance of the relationship of his head to his neck and of these to the rest of his body, and that by using his mind he could set up the situation least likely to interfere with optimum functioning. Eventually he discovered you could confine this experience by using the hands. Most of us are unaware how we use our bodies, even in making the most simple movements, but our body use contains an obvious account of all the basic habits we have taken on over the years. By continuously moving or keeping still in certain ways we gradually alter our body structure, and since we know that our muscles are linked to the part of our brain responsible for our conscious awareness of the world (as well as to the part which controls our actions) obviously the body actions affect the mind. If the body register is out of order, then the thinking process will be out of order as well. The mind and muscle tension are linked.

All kinds of things can produce muscle tension. A trauma

may have caused the muscles to contract in an unnatural way, or perhaps we have picked up a body device which fits in with the way we cope with a role we have chosen to play. We adopt attitudes in order to get on with other people. We have already seen, too, that an idea itself will set the muscles minutely into motion. There is a link between anxiety and muscle tension, so we can pick up a body stance appropriate for a particular emotional distress, and these tensions will become part of our posture. Without our knowing, our personal relationships are affected by the postures we have taken. Our whole nature is bound up with patterns of movement and posture. We are our posture.

Most people are misshapen somewhere through too much wrongly-distributed muscle-tension. We are all off-balance, twisted by over-contraction of certain muscles. The number of backaches and headaches suffered show just how much our body-wisdom has strayed. The problem is that most of us are encouraged to live perpetually off-balance, in a permanent condition of tiredness. We heap up tension upon tension to the point where we don't know we are misusing ourselves. The wrongness feels right. If, for example, your idea of having your arm out straight is really to have it tilted up a little, you can't order yourself to hold it in the right place because it feels wrong. We get attached to the old feelings of ourselves, and the distortions become the norm, so the balanced way may feel unreal.

This isn't just a question of good posture. We have lost our ability to come back to a place of rest and balance from which we can begin again with a balanced muscular control. We need this to reach a harmony and balance. Alexander didn't say we were all perfectly balanced naturally, and if we didn't interfere we would all be perfectly organised, but he did say we could choose to reach the best possible body functioning. His Principle was that if our body is out of kilter in its sense register then we must use our consciousness to re-educate the body. He wanted a way of reconstructing someone's life so he wouldn't be a victim of his past. Not by learning something new, but by unlearning the old. The process is complicated and teacher-training takes three years.

A teacher must learn to use himself as well as possible. For the client or 'pupil', this physical organisation of the body is an experiential and a mental experience. He is taught how he is misusing the body, when he is producing incorrect tension. By manual adjustment on the part of the teacher, he learns how to prevent this misuse. He also learns a 'body grammar', a new mental pattern in the form of series of words which he uses and learns to associate with new movements.

The most important point Alexander made was that we are all 'end-gainers'. Our education is such that we are persuaded into goals towards which we rush without seriously thinking about the best way to get there. Most of us act automatically. The impulse comes in, and out we rush to the goal without thinking whether the customary way of doing it is right. He said we must 'inhibit' this end-gaining. Once we receive the stimulus, there must be an 'inhibition' of the immediate muscle response so that by 'throughput' there can be adequate preparation for the next activity. The idea of inhibition was the foundation of his re-educating methods. A state of 'allowing' rather than 'doing', of a space for choice before the eventual muscle action and another period of activity. Not a passive state in case you make the wrong move, but an active state of rest. We misuse our bodies even in the simplest matters. There is good use and harmful use. By using the mind we can stand out of the way and let the right thing do itself.

In any movement there is a dynamic relationship of the body which will control the movement in the most efficient way, so we get maximum realisation from the minimum of effort. Even in the simplest movement, from the sitting to the standing position most people make more effort than is really required. You only have to watch people to realise how much effort is being used. What the teacher and also the pupil are doing is setting up the best psycho-physical (mind and body) conditions so there is least possible interference with the body's natural balance; to get an alignment which makes it possible to move efficiently with the least amount of effort. It is a process of lengthening the muscles to learn a better resting length.

The sitting to standing movement is often used as an example, not because it is important but because it is useful to understand the process. In this, the neck held free lets the head balance itself in a forwards-and-up direction from the spine. The weight of the head then allows the spine to lengthen and widen. The knees go forward and away. It is so subtle that it cannot really be seen, but the fourteen point weight of the head, forward and up in natural balance, acts as an anti-gravity mechanism to direct the body width, also forward and up. The muscles are extended. Muscles move by contraction so the more extension you have to begin a movement, the more potential you should have for the movement. With this physical set-up, the mind is thinking its direction and where to send the head when it is thinking 'stand'. It is thinking of the optimum conditions in the body. By directing and thinking of not interfering, i.e. 'inhibiting', you are then breaking your old habit patterns.

It is a complicated concept which would take a long time to study, but by setting up the optimum conditions in yourself, you maintain the optimum relationship of all parts of the body to themselves. You have mastered everything in yourself. You know the way you want to go and learn how not to interfere with the right response. This is a conscious way of letting the right thing happen through you, like a pianist who has a strict bodily discipline, who wills himself actively to play well. His object is to arrive at the point where he will play spontaneously; achieved spontaneity. Trying to do something makes the doing harder, but by letting things happen, allowing movement and rest, we have relaxed awareness. Like the birth of a baby or any creative output, the Will is set in motion and it should be left to itself to be born. As T.S. Eliot said "Teach us to care and not to care. Teach us to sit still."

The teaching process is complex and Isobel worked hard, but during the first year she didn't feel sensitive to what was happening. It felt good, but there was a sense of mystery; she was not connecting with what was actually happening. She caught a glimmer of what she was looking for, but she couldn't really sense what was going on. The main thing, she knew, was to build up experience of the process within herself and work from her own experience. But once the glimmer had come, it slowly dawned more and more. The more she allowed herself just to be aware through the contact with her hands, and not try to work things out, the more they happened. As Alexander taught, once something is set into motion, it will happen on its own.

It was the balance between 'allowing or being' and 'doing' that pleased her. Life is a process of expansion and contraction. Like breathing. When we breathe out, our breath reaches a peak and changes to become breathing in. There might be disturbances, a slowing of the breath, a loss of balance. Depending on what happens, what movement occurs, the rhythm will change. Sometimes it will be faster or slower, sometimes disturbed by some emotional or physical change. It brings an incredible variation of rhythm, but as long as there is life, the rhythm is constant. Our lives are both the extremes of a polarity and the balance between. We cannot have one side of the coin without the other, and if you forget that balance, you become stuck.

Alexander's was for Isobel the best system to bring the mind and body together in a direct way, by working with the body and at the same time affecting the habit patterns of thinking. But the more she worked, the more she felt a shift in her thinking. Most people came to Alexander lessons because it was the best system for sorting out physical problems. In this way the Technique was intellectually satisfying. They were also aware that if you are beginning to balance out the psycho-physical mechanism you are also beginning to balance out the whole person and a lot of things will right themselves. In re-educating the mind and body to a better way of being, it would seem natural that in the process many other things were sorting themselves out on the emotional and spiritual plane.

Isobel saw the principle of standing aside and letting things happen in relation to the whole personality. Gradually she began to translate the principle of good body use and changing habits and patterns of thinking to other levels of life. Depending on where the individual teacher is in his own process of growth, the principle can be taken further. "As long as my register is only on psycho-physical re-education, this is what will register in the pupil," says Isobel. "But the greater my conception of what wholeness is, the more than can happen through me. If my experience is keeping the various levels of being in balance: the emotional and spiritual as well as the mental and physical, then I can allow this understanding to come through me to my pupils. I can meet the person where they are. If they are at the level of having a headache and this is where they want to be, I will meet them on the psycho-physical level. If they are open to this being part of a pattern of the whole personality and recognise that the headache is only the issue that brought them along, that's fine. The thing is not to meet them where they are not."

The narrower the conception of awareness, the more the teacher will aim for a specific thing to set right. The wider his awareness the more general the balancing can be. If Isobel aims to balance the whole mechanism, then the specific thing will tend to itself. Her work is basically the same with everybody, but the particular thing that needs balancing will manifest in her sensitivity through the contact with her hands. "My experience in working was that there seemed to be a deeper layer beneath the disturbed area which knew what was right, and somehow I began to find by working for that deeper layer that I could evoke in the person a sense of the rightness in them, registering in their conscious, but not coming from their consciousness." Through her consciousness of the rightness, she was reaching the underlying part in the pupil that knew too, and allowing it to come through. She mediated and communicated this knowing to them.

The 'knowing' of the peak experience is perceiving right-ness, and once you emerge from the chaos surrounding that experience, you realise that the whole process of 'knowing' is given in order for you to accept the unknowing. Isobel particularly knew that major changes were taking place in her and was vaguely aware that she must allow them to take place without getting in touch with what was going on. In other words you realise the value of the unconscious as well as the conscious, and can trust that you are on a course of rightness without having constantly to know it consciously. The continuum is virtually an unconscious process; a state of unawareness in the way we use the world. Most 'growth' techniques emphasise the need for conscious awareness, and by saying awareness is good, they imply that unawareness is bad. Isobel began to realise that we are in danger of losing the value of our unconscious. She kicked against this constant concern with consciusness, with light and awareness, controlling and responsibility. As in all things we need a balance between awareness and unawareness. Consciousness can become routine, which means a loss of soul. The intellectual qualities have a habit of wearing off after a while. Consciousness couldn't cope with all the rich things going on in us. To go through life being totally aware, is almost anti-life, it becomes self-conscious to constantly inhibit and direct. Isobel felt there had to come a time when things should be left to happen automatically.

Knowing is a poor substitute for being, but it is only through consciously 'knowing' that you can know this. And it is only through her own conscious sense of rightness that Isobel now knows she can switch on to automatic on occasions, and doesn't have to keep repeating the process in a conscious way. It can now become, both for her and her pupil, an unconscious process. Neither need actually know what is happening, because she as the catalyst can automatically trigger the right thing in her pupils. "Every person is different, and even with the same person on a different occasion, it is a different experience. I use the physical framework of Alexander but I try to make it flexible. There isn't a typical session. Most Alexander teachers use the movement of sitting and standing as an example of the way you can both inhibit the habitual response and set up the new one in the new activity, but because I am aiming for something more than just the physical activity I don't use the same structure in the lesson. I try to bring out what is trying to happen in them, without going through the structure of a movement.

"I find now, more and more, I am listening with my hands to what is going on, trying to draw on a sense of what is already happening and directing that. Sometimes I am concentrating conciously on the process and guiding it quite consciously, and sometimes I am aware that something is going on, but I keep out of the way. Sometimes the pupil is aware of what is happening and sometimes not. Sometimes half and half. There are as many possible variations as you can have of a process of allowing and guiding. The more I understand the process the more consciously I am allowing the unconscious to hit a wider register. Because I have experienced some of the things myself I can recognise the importance of them.

"The whole issue of myself is that both sides, the conscious and the unconscious, have to be kept in balance, and one has to know when to use one and when the other. The way is to have these two totally available. The unconscious bringing information up, and the conscious meeting it there. As you trust more, you open more; the more you trust, the more happens. It is like a spiral of widening. As it becomes more subtle, my sensitivity is open to more subtle things."

Of course we need the light of our consciousness – the masculine in us – but to miss the importance of the dark unconscious feminine is to miss the point. It is a hard task, but if we are to balance our acute lopsidedness, the West must begin to realise this consciously.

What we lack, in ourselves as individuals and in society as a whole, is *The Feminine*.

4

The Heart of the Matter

"A stone is a slow dance, a flower a little faster. They are equal dances. There are no degrees in the dance of life only differences,"

Michael Adam

Down to Earth

"In the rose the Dance is wholly done,
but blindly done. It is in becoming
man that God now comes to consciousness
of himself and of that dance which he
does elsewhere unconsciously, simply
out of his nature as a dancer."

Michael Adam

Life is constant movement. Like the compass, it swings. If we become lopsided, it must swing towards balance. It is yin and yang, male and female, light and dark. It is the nature of change. We hold everything within us. There is a totality available to every human being. We are mind and feeling, sensation and intuition. We are both rational and non-rational, neither wholly masculine nor wholly feminine. We each of us hold the masculine elements of fire and air: of focus, division and change, and also the feminine elements of earth and water: of the fixed, the accepted and an awareness of the unity of all life. We are each of us able to live in the realm of the heart and the head. As Irene Claremont de Castillejo says, we are equally capable of the masculine focused consiousness and the feminine diffuse awareness. For a woman everything is enjoyed as a whole, she does not need to analyse, she is just aware. For a man to be aware is not enough. He must learn about everything that comes to him.

Swedenborg said the masculine represents love of truth, the feminine the truth of love. Logos in terms of vocation. Eros in human relationships. It is woman's consciousness to spread out and men's to focus. Unless we find a balance between the two, we miss much in our lives.

For a girl it is obvious from the beginning that inter-relationships are very important – more than for a boy. For the boy to develop his masculinity he must move away from the nursery, and strike out against the parent god. A girl must grow away too, but she can do so parallel to, and within the relationship of the family. The nursery provides the pattern of the feminine through the mother. It is in the home that she first tries out her feminity with the otherness of the important male, the father figure. Adolescence brings in the aspect of the sexual playmate, during which a girl begins to try out her femaleness and establish it against the otherness of the masculine which isn't her father. She anchors in her innate sexuality and sensuality. This is primitive woman, who lives and feels what she is, and it is in her that man senses his feminine soul and wants to be united with it.

The female part in a man's unconcious was called by Jung, the 'anima'. The anima is the female archetype in each man, the collective picture of primitive woman as she has appeared through centuries of human experience in relation to man. The alluring, attractive and treacherous female of myth to whom the hero is strongly attracted. It is the personification of all feminine psychological traits in man's psyche: his vague feelings and moods, his interest in the non-rational, his feeling for nature and ability to love. It is also his relation to the unconscious.

Woman has always represented man's unknown female soul because he has never been complete in himself. Because he is unconsciously looking for the female to make him more whole, when he first meets a woman he likes, he projects his anima on to her. He is not relating to the woman herself but to his unconscious idea of what a woman should be. This has nothing to do with his own experience, but with all the collective experience that man has ever had, and which is lying in his unconscious. It is the primitive, instinctive female in all men, and since this is a distortion, it makes him see the woman as more pefect than she really is. A repressed anima and the ideas he has gathered from his experience with his mother and other women, will give a completely false picture about the actual woman he has met. It is as though half of himself is in the woman, and for this reason she becomes necessary as well as fascinating. By relating to her, he is relating to his own soul which he can't find in any other way.

In her naive, primitive feminity, the woman is like a mirror image. The man can see, through her, his own inner, non-rational being and his half unrealised feelings. The woman who is at the primitive, instinctive anima stage can be so unconsciously aware of this that she may even reflect his mood before he is aware of it himself. The anima in his unconscious, connected to aspects not developed, is likely to be childish. When something upsets him to the point where reason and control are submerged, the anima will show itself in a silly emotional way. But if the female in man can be detached from the collective archetype and brought into consciousness, the feminine will add depth to a man's character. For a man to discover the feminine side of his own nature, is not to make him more feminine, but more truly masculine. It sets him free to be himself. He has the analysing, deductive view of life, but can also use the heart values. He can think through organisation in human terms and not build huge structures in which the individual gets lost. It offers a new dimension in creativity, which is urgently needed as the huge, unwieldy, impersonal organisations begin to crumble. It also means he can relate in a more rewarding way to the women he meets in his life. He will acquire a greater capacity for loving, without being sentimental. Instead of being disappointed by his anima projection, he will be able to relate more harmoniously.

If a woman becomes stuck in the role of sexual playmate, the unconscious primitive female, she can go on in this way for years, into her forties or fifties. She can use this role to bind any man that comes her way and hold him back. The feminine principle is the matrix of life from which the seed springs. She holds the fixed, eternal qualities of the earth, she is nourishing and regenerating. But she is also unpredictable. She can unite, but in the unconscious she can also bind. The all-female female can become demanding and self-seeking and childish. Unconsciously she can subtly bind her children and make them feel constantly guilty. She can emasculate her sons so they feel insecure and make her daughters insecure as women.

The male aspect in the unconscious of women was called by Jung the 'animus' and the projection of this, the collective picture of primitive, instinctive man, is caught by the men she meets in a relationship. She, too, projects an important part of her unconscious on to him and is then fascinated or put off by what she sees in him. But if a woman can understand the wholeness of her nature and find the masculine within herself, it sets her free to be more human, less protective and aggressive. If she stops looking outside herself for direction and purpose, she can direct her own non-rational, emotional and intuitive nature. She is free to be what she is.

Over centuries of history, humanity has become increasingly masculine. This was necessary to bring humanity into consciousness. We had to come away from the unity of primitive instinct to become ego-conscious. To understand humanity, we had to divide and separate the world into its component parts. The world cannot run itself. Without a certain amount of order and structure and authority, there would be chaos. But with this emphasis our education has pushed us into lopsidedness; we have lost the basis of human relationship, represented first by our relationship with our own mother. Women have been caught up in a male-oriented ego-conscious world, but ironically until recently they have been forced by men to remain behind in the role of primitive woman.

But women are not instinct only. They are more than the simple urges that nature gave us. It is the nature of humanity to evolve from the primitive, instinctual phase of innocence through to ego consciousness. And this includes woman. This need obviously brought women into conflict and as we have seen, it is conflict that leads to consciousness. To survive, women were forced to set their will into action. In the last few years women have been extricating themselves with great friction from the femine role forced on them by the circumstances of history. To earn new self-respect and independence, they have been forced to come up from their natural place in the darkness of the unconscious and make themselves fully conscious. They have had to become individuals in their own right and to do this have had to come out into the world of men and take back responsibility for their own masculinity. They have forcibly taken back responsibility for their own masculine soul – their other half – and assimilated him into their own personality.

Over the last few years, women have come into contact with the lesser-known reasoning side of their nature and begun to behave on a more impersonal basis. Since the masculine quality of consciousness is out in the world, she has had the means readily at hand to take responsibility for her own animus. Her realisations about life have always been in the feeling realm but now, with the help of the animus, she has found the ability to focus it. Focusing is not the same as thinking – which is a function we all have. Feelings can't be used in a positive way, unless we have a way of hanging on to the sadness or joy to produce it in a creative way. Ideas come to everyone, but men have the more natural ability to focus on them. It is this which makes man a creative being. Although the animus in a woman has the same ability, since it is in the unconscious it is attained in an indirect way. The unconscious is unlimited, but you can't create until some limits are set. With focus a woman can analyse, choose and give form to her feelings.

At the primitive stage, the ego of a woman hides in the unconscious and she gets what she wants indirectly through her man. But now, since she has been forced to make her own way in the competitive work world, the world in which men are more at home, she can come into consciousness for herself. She can work directly for what she wants. This gives her more self-respect. As she moves from the primitive stage of innocence to the second stage of sophistication, her personality develops. But for some women a developed animus means getting on in life using masculine qualities, and they like this personal power. Evolution doesn't regress, but as with everything we must beware of rigidity. There is a danger of becoming stuck. It was a necessary part of evolution for women to become conscious, but as with all emerging energies, the consciousness had to come in an exaggerated form before it could be refined. The suffragettes paved the way for a new attitude by and towards women, and more recently the women's movements have taken up the fight. But when an archetype comes up from the dark, it has a tendency to take over. When the non-habitual in the unconscious tries to take over, it becomes distorted.

The women's movements have gone over the top. They are animus possessed. By adopting excessive masculine qualities, the women have been pushed into becoming men. No longer guided by the feminine impulse, a woman's opinions and rationalisations can become dogmatic. She produces cold reasoning that does not come from the place a woman is at in herself. Though it seems logically thought out, it is not true wisdom at all. The exaggeration has been necessary to bring the right energy through, but in these terms it has not yet produced balance and integration. Woman's Liberation has been pushing down the femine and perpetuating further the materialistic, unfeeling world of men. The women in this movement are also identifying with the power of knowledge. No longer guided by the feminine, the personal ego is identified with the animus, the primitive man who overdoes things and then collapses.

To find her independence modern woman had to go out into the world of men, but she also had to sacrifice her emotional life to it. This has caused confusion because something is missing, and she knows it. She has been pulled away from her primitive instinct, out of necessity, but she can't quite let go her tie with the mother earth from which she came. By bringing the masculine side of her nature into a proper balance, a woman can become more wholly female. By focusing her mind clearly on her emotions and objectively analysing what she is doing and why, in a kind of constant inward meditation, she can present her own non-rational functions of feeling and intuition in a more directed, useful way. Psychological development is watching and analysing instinctive reactions. It is looking at the working of nature and presenting it in an understandable way. You can consciously see what life wants of you. To be conscious of that instinctive behaviour you begin to find within yourself, the part of you which is not personal ego. The awareness comes in of a new value, an inner truth that used to be expressed by religion, but which we had to lose while we went through an age of consciousness, dominated by the ego. As the pendulum swings back towards a balance, it is woman's evolutionary pattern to regain her link with nature and mother earth. The combination of instinct and focus (or self-consciousness) allows the instinct to reappear with insight.

For the female it is natural to live within the unconscious movements of the earth. She is closely in touch with the rhythms of nature. She is tied to the power of the earth and linked exclusively with the Great Mother Goddess. The mythical figure of the mother represents our origins; first our actual mother and our origin as a particular individual, but also of the earth itself from which all life seems to spring. Myth was the language in which the psychological processes, common to every man no matter what culture, were described. Every god in myth represents the spiritual aspect of instinct in the biological sense. The old primitive Mother Goddess represented pure femininity, the most basic, elemental, emotional femine which stirs in us. There are two aspects to her. One the benevolent, cherishing, nourishing and protective side of the earth mother. The other, its treacherous, negative aspect which was the engulfing, overpowering side. The Great Mother is concerned with love in all its connotations; she is a total benefactress who wants to take in everything that needs love and comfort. But she is also jealous and vain.

In Egypt in 4000-2000 BC, the Age of Taurus, the gods were in the power of nature and everything in nature. Represented by the Great Mother, the age valued femininity and infinite fertility. Culture in the Taurean Age brought in the new consciousness of fertility of the earth and concern

159

with the livingness of life. The great discovery of the Age was that if you planted seeds, they would grow. And the link between Taurus and its opposite sign of Scorpio, indicated that God was in sexuality. The miracle of life was procreation and it became divine because people couldn't understand it biologically. It was the only age with two fixed astrological signs signifying the feminine pole, in which the feminine was valued, and in this matriarchal culture it became overhauled.

The feminine came to power in the Taurean Age, but in the Arian age it was completely beaten down. The Age of Aries became a patriarchy. The migrants from Scandinavia and the Baltic invaded the agricultural culture right down to its Mediterranean base. They toppled the culture and settled. With the warriors came male gods. All the mythical matriarchal figures were married off and became shadows of their husbands. The rights of the mother now became secondary to the rights of Zeus, Apollo and the Olympian deities. Gods anthropomorphised in human forms, where before they were unformed or half-animal, bestial characters. In the Age of Pisces the feminine completely disintegrated. Divine Right now passed through the male line instead of the female. It also brought in the male religions such as Judaism with the misogynist patriarchal god, Jehovah. Frightened by the power of the matriarchy, the new ages overcompensated furiously and the feminine crashed violently. In Christianity a father figure produces a son, not in myth, but divinely human. The father and son became a collective religious experience and the Mother Goddess was repressed and forgotten. She appeared again later in the cult of the Virgin Mary, but only in the purest form of womanhood. She was only acceptable if man approved, and if she behaved. There was no way man could allow the dark aspect of her nature.

In its negative form it is the feminine that steals energy from the collective unconscious and causes depression and the atmosphere of inertia. She becomes a witch. Stuck in the dark in the unconscious unable to make the necessary step in evolution to meet the situation, she will do what every female does when her path is thwarted; she will become the spoilt female who mars her man's pleasure by saying 'no'. When the true feminine, the dark aspect of nature, is ignored, she will cause havoc and fight for recognition. When she's being pushed into the background, she will come out with all her power and use it negatively. The unconscious causes disturbance so that it may become integrated into the ego. The goal of the Mother Goddess, as Marie Von Franz says, is to become human, to produce a human daughter. The dark aspect of the old Mother Goddess has still to appear, transformed in consciousness in our civilisation. The New Aquarian Age, 'with its Leo polarity, has something of the fixed feminine pole of the Taurean Age. It indicates a seeking of the centre, the mystery at the heart of things.

As the seed which pushes upwards, the dark will always strive to go to the light. Everything dark pushes hard from underneath to re-establish balance. And anything in the light too long will try to move to the dark before it becomes desiccated by too much sun. It was necessary for Western man to ignore the Mother Goddess for a while and to place emphasis on the male development of ego-conciousness. But now she feels hurt and ignored, and when the hurt is ignored, the door is open to animus attacks. Animus possession is the hurt woman, a camouflaged cry for love, but in the way a woman does, it says it doesn't want the thing it wants most, because it wants to hurt the thing which has hurt it.

Working like men, women cannot feel completely happy, because in the focused, separative world of men, a woman cannot work from the heart of her being. Her emotional nature is in limbo. To make her way in the outside world of men, she has to cling to what she has achieved through the intellect. If she lets go, she will sink like a stone, drop back into just being nature once again. So many women are frightened to give up their work because the pull of the primitive towards inertia is very strong. They dare not give up in case they become cabbage-like. It takes a tremendous effort to get away from that pull, the regressive inertia of the feminine, and not to follow the old pattern. If the animus isn't very strong a woman can vegetate in the typical way of the feminine. It may be easier to follow the daily routine, but it lacks all the excitements of life.

Because she needs to go out in a conscious way and protest openly against all instinctive feelings, quite often she has to shut off her sexuality. She identifies with the male way of the impersonal and pushes her femininity into the unconscious. This can only make her more confused and unhappy. To survive she must grow and yet again she is willed into action. No amount of facts will make a woman experience the non-ego values of a higher Self, it is only through experiencing her own nature that she can relate to this – the Feminine Principle itself. The feminine principle is the relatedness of things, not factual knowledge and wisdom. A woman needs her animus so she isn't trodden on and then the primitive woman, transformed by consciousness, can behave in a positive way. She provides the path to the spirit. Becoming conscious by self-analysis, she becomes conscious of the path of rightness. By being right inwardly, the problems of the world can resolve themselves. Such is the uncanny power of the unconscious. By being right in herself about a problem, the outside falls in place too. She will know intuitively what is right. The feminine principle is to attain a subtle rightness. Knowing is the realisation that something is going on and submitting to it She needs her animus to light up, like a torch, what she instinctively knows, so she knows she knows it.

In the evolutionary process we are all trying to get away from the primitive mother in personal as well as collective terms. What is chasing us most is our mothers. We have to struggle for independence, so we can come to ego consciousness. None of us is free from the influence of our parents' unconscious, but since through circumstances women have been in greater need, it is relevant that they have fought harder to loosen the grip of the mother's primitive unconscious; in a way more difficult because of the unbroken line between mother and daughter. The mother may seem quite gentle, but in her unconscious she may be very strong. Quite unknowingly she can tie you up because you cannot risk displeasing her. Consequently she unconsciously stops you relating properly to men. As Diana says, "all my life I was fighting to get away from my mother. For many years I was desperate for her approval and reinforcement and to get away I had to let go of my need for that. Only recently, as I let go of needing her, she stopped being negative. Assagioli told me that the greatest gift my mother gave me was a traumatic childhood. I went through the whole gamut of human emotions possible because of my mother." By accepting the existence of that destructive pull, it loses its power.

In consciousness, the mother cannot cloy or destroy. A subpersonality is frustrated and can become a nuisance, but when it is recognised, accepted and given what it needs, its higher value can come through. Women hurt by their mother's negative animus, lack the security that more positive mothers were able to give their children, but in fighting their way through to an understanding of what was happening, they were forced to experience the spiritual meaning of life. It is now our personal role to get away from the mother and to repossess the positive feminine power. By accepting it consciously, it no longer has personal power.

Women today have been 'fortunate' in being forced through necessity into this initial thrust for identity, and therefore into greater psychological development. The Will had to be set into motion for this inevitable fight, but men have not yet had to do this. Already in ego-consciousness, man has not had to fight. He has not had to face up to the fact that he too is caught up in the primitive female energy. Until he realises this and takes responsibility for his own unconscious female, and is prepared to integrate this into a properly balanced male energy, he will continue to relate wrongly.

As women continue to develop psychologically, in a very new way, this becomes more and more apparent. Men have been leading us quite happily in the way of the mind, and because of this they haven't yet needed to use their Will towards new psychological growth. For the most part, then, they remain unaware of the new kind of emotional and spiritual satisfaction that women are beginning to need. All they know is that things aren't what they used to be in relationships, and are consequently confused. This is why increasingly women have begun to find comfort and emotional rapport in relation to each other. Focusing on feelings and making all reactions conscious it is possible to have a far deeper psychological relationship.

There is excitement in mutual discovery of a new emotional development, and an increasing dissatisfaction with 'intellectual' conversations in which the feeling in things is never talked about. To a woman these are only words, expressing the situation in a logical, deductive sense. By finding their masculine in the world of work, as M. Esther Harding says, women are moving away from the collective values of being wife and mother, simply representing their husband's soul, instead of being individuals in their own right. But men are still trying to make the old types of relationship with collective values and little awareness of true relationship in a partnership. Women have found these new values of relationship for themselves and want to bring them into their relationships with men, but men haven't learned the lesson yet. So a woman can relate more totally to another woman, emotionally, psychologically and often mentally as well. They are part of the same process and the experiences are similar. It provides a sameness, not a mirror reverse as it does with a man. To help understand yourself, you can see other aspects of the female in another woman. You can see how the physical could be included as a natural extension of the ability to relate totally.

It is an important relationship, but its exclusitivity can only be a temporary phase, a mood we are passing through in individual development. In the biological sense, women are going backwards, but psychologically they are progressing. It is as though the biological urge is satisfied and the emphasis is now on the psychological urge. The stage may be necessary to further humanity. But too much sameness is not a good thing. Woman need the creative tension of the polar opposite which can never be found in a woman. This may appear to be found because women are relating to the masculine side of the other woman, but as we swing back to balance, the need to relate to a woman will subside. We will relate to men in a more balanced, beneficial and life-enhancing way.

Women more than men are beginning to understand that relationships can only take place when each person is standing opposite, not entangled with the other. Each person must be allowed his own space in which to progress and grow, safeguarded from destructive projections and illusions. Women's task is to bring the feminine values to reality in a real world. Men must find their feminine before relationships can be made once again on an equal but separate basis. The need for the emotional and spiritual of the female and the mental and physical of the male is vital, but eventually we should be able to swing across to meet in the middle too. It should be possible for women to relate in the men's sphere of the mind and men to relate in the women's sphere, yet keeping their own ground, with all options open. Like two sides of a river with an occasional bridge between.

Feeling is a woman's world and it is not surprising that men hesitate to leave the sphere in which they feel secure. For the female to gain her maleness is an outward process, a question of finding her outer personality. The Saturn hit around twenty-one meant for the most part a breaking up of old values, but in the outside world. It triggered the need to take possession of the animus which, although difficult, meant fighting in the light. The Saturn hit at twenty-nine was an inner breaking up. To acquire the renewed feminine, a woman has to go within. If that journey is frightening for her, who is most at home in the dark of the unconscious, how much more must it be for a man!

The female is holding the male on an unconscious level and restricting him, and for a man to find his femaleness is an inner task, an inner journey into the dark and unconscious realms. The path is through his emotions. The anima in man entangles him in life and its problems, forcing him to deal with instincts and drives. He has to revise his whole religious attitude to life. The loneliness and isolation are hard, but the unconscious must always be experienced in isolation before you can return to life.

To find the female is the task of both men and women. A frightening challenge for the bravest hero.

Up to Earth

"We move out of innocence and animal grace,
out of blindly being God
into the gaucherie of seeming only man;
it is up to us then to move into that grace
again that comes of being awaredly God."

Michael Adam

The world, though dominated by the masculine, is in chaos through loss of manhood. There is very little real male energy because the Earth Mother has been blocking it. The more unconscious the mother, the more destructive her power, and the way of the negative female is chaos. Wrong male energy has brought lack of direction, because the male is unable to perform his rightful function of structure and organisation. We are caught by female inertia and doing nothing. For most men, the male soul is unconscious and inacccessible, so integrating the female into their psyche is the only way for men to retrieve their maleness. The path passes through their emotions and, as Jung said, the least-developed function in anyone's psyche is like a demon of mischief when it tries to come through. Those few men who have done so have gone through hell.

Because the female is in her rightful place in the unconscious she can bring up her own femaleness more easily, although she can free the man to find his own energy pattern.

By understanding this in consciousness, the effect will be felt below the level of apparent consciousness. By being open herself, she can influence her man unconsciously. Freed from the binding link between them, a man's energy will find balance. While the mother is holding the son, the daughter finds it difficult to receive the son. He is not free. By releasing the tie of the mother (and of course the father) on a conscious level, you become free on the more unconscious level. We never want to be totally free from the continuum mother, but to be conscious enough to release the mother's hold. By doing this women will also be released to receive, which is their rightful function. This is the female contribution to consciousness.

The female is a receiver. The male the perceiver. A concept more easily understood if you think of an eye. We do not perceive with the eyes, but with the mind. The eye is the organ of reception (the female). The mind is the perception (the male). The eye ordinarily trusts the mind to discriminate what it sees, and if it can have this trust the organ is free to take in anything without any discrimination at the point of seeing. The mind can do the discriminating. The same applies to the male and female in each of us. The female has learned not to trust the male to discriminate and so protects itself at the eye. The female is holding the male. The eye (female) is trying to do the discriminating and perceiving, as well as the receiving, and consequently usurps the mind (male) and leaves male no power. The only thing left to him is to control the female. He will only allow her to see what he wants her to see.

Brought in in a new way, with no man waiting for her, the female will create hell until a man is brought through for her. The female has first to let go of the male. Before the male can stop controlling her, she must stop possessing on the old subconscious level. When the female is brought to femaleness in a new way, we have to raise the male in a new way as a perceptive organ rather than a controlling one, and allow the female again to be receptive and responsive. The primal male and female functions can then be freed to combine in a new way, and to understand the interaction in a totally different sense. If we can withdraw the mind from the body and say 'I trust you to receive, the mind is here to discriminate', the instinctive behaviour of the female can go on. Woman has been withdrawing from the male. She has been getting into her knowing and into her proper power to make it possible for a new phase to come about. Women's Liberation was concerned with separating, because we have to become separate before we can unite. The movement symbolised externally what 'knowing woman' has been doing in a quieter way, and proved the energy for the 'knowing woman'. She has been given a certain amount of freedom because of this.

A female power is coming through, but we could easily misuse it, as we now misuse the male energy. An overemphasis of the male was necessary for the female to be brought back – at its extreme an opposite becomes its own contrast. We must now be careful to make sure that the power of the female is not taken further than is needed to hold the balance. In the Taurean age the female was unconscious and consequently easily became over-emphasised. Now the female has to be made conscious in order that we can be aware of not allowing either 'knowing' (awareness of the unconscious) or consciousness to get out of balance. We have to have consciousness of the unconscious to understand the balance between them.

To understand this balance we have now to accept the dark, unconscious side within each of us. We must take back the responsibility for darkness and evil that we have projected outside us into the cosmos. We should realise our own potential for misusing the male or female consciousness, and claim back all the archetypes which we project outside ourselves. Instead of projecting the dark forces out into some other source, we should now recognise the real live demon inside us. By accepting that we are capable of the worst deeds, we are given the choice. And by claiming these evils, we weaken their power. By projecting them out, as the male religions have done, the evils are created and become a real force. The more the dangers are rejected and pushed out, the greater the power we give to them. We now have to accept responsibility. We are God and the Devil, good and evil.

Within us is potential for both, but evil is only evil in the way it is expressed. In terms of the Earth Mother, for example, she is only one force, a feminine force, but she can be used for good or bad. If we accept that she is a powerful force, we can choose whether she should be a force for enrichment and grounding, or a force for manipulation and destruction. And we can either see male consciousness as a beneficent force for directing, focusing and understanding the way life is, or we can use it for repressing, controlling and denying the importance of the instincts of the female.

There are many people looking in this direction, who in searching for a new religion, have jumped on a bandwagon. They have been searching for a spiritual path and this has led to a growth in occult activities. It began with the drug culture. People have got caught up with Eastern philosophies and growth techniques derived from these, and are persuaded that they need to transcend. If it is spiritual, it must be right because we all know we are spiritual. But there is also a danger. The Eastern way is to completely withdraw from physical phenomena and retreat into the inner being, but this is not particularly suited to the mind and make-up of Western man. The Eastern way has this world is an illusion and has to be transcended. The Christian ethic too has led us to believe that we are born in original sin and must get away from it, and that when we die, we can go 'out there'. We need now to find the mystery of the spirit not in isolation from the physical world, but hidden in the material form, and to find the spiritual behind the physical.

The Alchemists said that "what is above is like that which is below, and what is below is like that which is above. And as all things have come from One by the meditation of One, all things have been born from this single thing. The oneness arises from the earth to the sky and again descends to the earth." Spirit-matter. Mind-body. Male-female. Microcosm-macrocosm. Each is a reflection of the other. Primitive cultures were in touch with the instincts of the body and in the Taurean Age spirit was in matter. Masculine consciousness is by nature directed outward and it is the male way to go up, out of the body, to find the spiritual world. Women too, caught up in their animus can also go up through the mind, the male way. There are two paths, and if she misses the path to earth, a woman can go to the sky, a mirror of the earth, in spite of the warning her head gives her. People think the male god principle is to do with the spiritual, and the mother goddess is to do with fertility of crops. But both are in each. If a girl falls into the animus and is overwhelmed by the unconscious, she can get entangled with spiritual nasties. Some people break out of themselves in such a way that they lose control of themselves. They see things in such a chaotic way that they have no control over themselves. The visions flood them and become a source of mental illness. By coming to consciousness and humanness, the woman can avoid this.

Going to God is to go to the highest thing, but it is automatically to go to the lowest too. We have been driving upward for consciousness and enlightenment, and the need to be earthed has been forgotten. But women are discovering that life is hollow when the animus is no longer satisfying, because they have lost touch with their basic physical selves. By being really in our body we are also in touch with the spirit. The physical body repeats the pattern of all other stages. The original contains all the others. If matter is made up of spirit, matter contains all the stages of existence.

In terms of Isobel's body work, we have turned our bodies (the female) into a controlling thing and people have begun to sense things out of their bodies. If the mind comes together and stops controlling the body, the conscious can then take control of the unconscious. At the moment the mind is tying up energy by controlling the body and not allowing it to receive. Things have gone wrong in terms of the continuum, we have lost our sense of well-being in the body. Men stick in their mental bodies and attitudes and although the drug culture blew a few minds, the physical bodies are not actually functioning. It is a question of loosening minds, not the bodies – although in life's constant paradox it is the opposite too. Consciousness goes up and out, the unconscious goes down and in. In altered states of consciousness, men will go up towards the spirit. Women can go up too, but also by being themselves in a more conscious way, women know they have the balance of spirit and matter within them. With the help of their animus women make contact with the female soul. They have to take the conflict out of their minds and sift it through their bodies in order to create.

Women can find the spiritual in a being way. It is easier for them to be themselves than it is for men because women can only be what they are. Men must do it in a doing way. They must work in a more conscious way to bring the spirit and body back into harmony. When men were organising their religions, it was natural for them to look out to the spiritual in the universe. It is man's way to project outwards in prayer and meditation. Women draw down that energy before projecting it out for good. But with the return of the feminine principle, both men and women can now find the female god within. They need not project out but in. Man is God. We are all in our bodies. No one need go out of their body. We can find everything there is inside us. We are the counterpart of God, not the manifestation, but the source. And inside our bodies we are safer. Our bodies are stable. The people who fly out in spirit, have made that outer spiritual world a reality. There is no need to go off into frightening realms. If you find the spirit within the body, it is under your control. Meditation is being in touch with yourself. It is diffuse awareness. It is not irrelevant that growth techniques have so far been initiated by men. Focusing on a centre is a male thing, which of course has value, but being aware of yourself is also meditation. Life is a meditation on yourself.

If matter is a manifestation of spirit, we can find spirit by going more deeply into matter. This must contain the soul. The further you go into physical matter, into yourself, the more the opposite can happen. To go through matter, to the heart of the matter, is to experience other realities. By going into the atom, you go into the cosmos. There is no value in being out of the body. As Isobel says, we need to be in our body totally, not locked so tightly that we have no possibility of experiencing anything, but to be at ease in our body. To possess the body, but not to be possessed by it. Not to hold it and control it as men are doing. We can experience other realities by being ourselves, and knowing it.

The deeper we go into matter and the greater the sense of allowing the unconscious to vibrate, the more attuned we become to spirit. As the tuning becomes more subtle, the greater the sensitivity to subtlety. The more in tune with the cosmos, the sense of the link between the microcosm and the macrocosm. Your mood can be in tune with the universe. You can sense the energies in stones, or be aware of the phases of the moon. At the point where you are wholly in touch with yourself you are wholly in touch with the universe. At whatever level of growth, whether we are reaching some kind of balance in our emotional, physical or mental nature, everything must be related back to the body. Isobel describes her work as making a connection between the outer and inner parts of a person's psyche and tying their experience back down into the deep self, back into the female. Expanding along the spiritual path in order to cope with emotions does not work, as Liz discovered, unless all the elements are tied down to earth. We have to be able to relate to Self totally before relating totally to anything else in the right way.

It is our business to try and live our lives, to express what we have been given. As Isobel says, in her work she cannot take anyone anywhere she hasn't been herself, but having said that, by being in touch with her own earth, she is in a sense in touch with everything and can take anyone anywhere. She can bring them in touch with that continuum by being in touch with it herself. By being open yourself, the channel is clear to bring the spirit down, through to earth. You can jump into the continuum, like the stream of real life which carries us along in its current. Through greater earthing, we can then go higher.

The more into matter, the more into spirit. The more we understand the manifestation, the closer we come to that which is being manifest. We are a higher Self choosing to have a body and if we are not really in touch with that deep lower self, we are missing the point. The body is in touch with the rhythms of nature and the greatest poverty is not to live in this world. The metaphysical is good only if it is brought into our daily lives. The personality is our workshop. This 'isness' is all we have. If we try to gain the higher Self we shall lose it. But if we carry on being our personality, our personality will be so attractive, the higher self will come down to see what we are about. You cannot transcend physical reality until you are actually in touch with it. If you are not properly in touch, the spiritual realities you see are real, but your awareness is off-key. Everything you perceive will be off-centre. If you are truly in touch with the nature of things, then your perspective is cleared. There are gods and hierarchies out in the cosmos for some people but for the majority of us this is not our trip. Some people are flying out in the energy or etheric body, but to bring their flights of fancy down they must come back to base. If people can get all aspects of their personality, the mind, body and emotions into some kind of balance, they will automatically be led towards the spiritual with all the parts at ease with each other. But if people move out of their physical bodies into the energy body, through meditation, peak experiences or sexuality, because their mind, body and feelings are giving them trouble they become caught up in the parts and are not working them out. You can step out of reality and move into this other realm to get a more complete picture of yourself but a lot of people are left split up, sitting outside themselves. Most people come back automatically through everyday realities, but there is a risk of needing to spend more and more time outside because it seems more comfortable and emotionally exciting.

We tend to think that if the male is only going up, the woman is only going down. But all actions have the opposite going on as well. The female is not only going down into herself, but is bringing her unconscious up again to earth. The male is not only going up to the spirit but is bringing it down to earth. The flow is a coming together and meeting, but in a more conscious knowing. We must be more aware of both ends of the spectrum, and of the greater use of the whole unconscious, intuitive faculties which will be used in a lightened way. The unconscious will be more available, in a lighter, happier, sillier way. We won't just have experience of other realities, but will be balanced by being on earth in the here and now. Sometimes we will be content to be happy and although aware of the links with nature as we are living within it, need not be searching around for something else. This is the polarity. It is back up to earth on earth.

If men are to continue going up to find their spirituality, they will go up alone. If they will do so by coming down then the spirit, their soul, can be mediated to them by a woman. We have to go through our opposite. A man can either go through his female consciousness to find his male God, or through the female unconscious of the conscious, knowing woman he can reach his male soul. The masculine is forward looking and his way is to go forward into consciousness. The female can look back. And by going forward she is going back. Humanity can go up into the spiritual, but to do so is to leave out the importance of matter and of the unconscious. If we are constantly aware of the higher self and try to line everything up with it, a whole side of our being is negated. We are confused into thinking that if there is a higher self, it has to be better, and that we must consciously try to get there and hold it. But we cannot have continuous daylight. To want everything to be conscious implies we must escape from our inner nature and that God is all light. As the bible says, if we try to save the soul we shall lose it. If we cling to hope then we are holding it. It is by giving up hope that things may happen. When we don't need security, we can have it. It is a difficult lesson in this materialistic age. The paradox of letting go, is that we have to become conscious before we can let go and allow ourselves to be unconscious again. By finding the tangles in the unconscious and clearing the knots consciously to make a connecting thread with the higher Self, we can put positive symbols back down. The unconscious isn't just a cesspool, it has far greater richness. Let us keep that mystery. Our creativity comes from there and we need to be in contact with that very deep layer. If we want to understand an artist we can do so through his work, through the manifestation of what he is trying to express. We see it more clearly than if we try to understand his abstract ideas. The 'growth movement' with its awareness techniques says we have to know, to be conscious. In this quantum leap a new thing is happening between the conscious and the unconscious. When the two meet something new happens. We have consciousness of the unconscious.

There are always opposing functions in everything and both are right, or at least have their rightness when brought together. The whole concept of male/female, conscious/unconscious is to put them together and keep each one, so neither is competing but existing together in conscious co-operation. Neither is good or bad. This operates this way and that operates that way, but both operate together. If each one is doing the right thing, we find the rightness in ourselves. We can relate again to the male and female in other people with a sense of rightness. There is a more complete relationship, but also a more rightful one. Each one being totally what he is, held in balance with the other. It is a dance between the conscious and the unconscious. We have the masculine warp and weft and now we have the feminine needle weaving the colour in between. The space between is potential movement. Somehow who-I-am is the dance, not my conscious or unconscious. Not the higher or the instinctual self, but the dance between them. Who-I-am is the expression and the expression is the importance. As long as they are static, neither will work. When there is movement, expression, flow and growth, that is when I exist. Neither knowing or not knowing. Woman, living in a conscious age, but naturally in touch with the unconscious, has come to a point where the higher Self is for a moment in balance with the personality – and that is the point of knowing. It is held registered in the conscious, but also in the unconscious. The conscious knowing is the moment of 'isness' between instinct and our consciousness of it. Then it must be let go, to start again and find new balance on another level.

Knowing says you have to let go. By grabbing the conscious you are holding the feminine back. But being yourself, by being human, you become a human-being. Life means growth and change. The process is like pregnancy and giving birth. You do it in good faith, although you have no idea where it is coming from. Your concern is for the child and the growth taking place, but you don't want to mess it up. This is a time for the unknown. Life can be cleared through on many levels and these might come to light later on. Consciousness should be an aid to the unconscious, but not take it over. Once the baby is born, then there is a whole stage of knowing. The balance must be constant. Some things are better unknown.

Knowing says you have to take the right way and let things happen, because you cannot see where you are going. Our consciousness wants to know where it is going before we start, to see the light at the other end of the tunnel. But there is no end. Man can embody truth, but he cannot know it, said W.B. Yeats. We must be our philosophy rather than do it. We must allow the growth to settle and anchor and earth. The female embodies time. In myth it is man who can get things done in a moment. The woman must sow shrubs for seven years. Time is the essential factor and nothing else can help. Women, now conscious, can get things done. Men, who must find their unconscious, have no time limit. The inner woman in man will wake up in her own time.

The Holy Grail

We say God and the imagination are one.
How high that highest candle lights the dark ... '

Wallace Stevens

To hold the opposites together is the most difficult job in a
world where the opposites are so far apart. The instinctive
female earth nature of man has to be set free and guided, not
educated and controlled. It has to be acknowledged and held
in balance. Men have now to work themselves down from
focused consciousness into the diffuse awareness of the
unconscious. For 'knowing woman' the knowing comes in
consciousness; it happens where the masculine and feminine
meet. A spark goes across and the woman registers it in
consciousness. She knows. But it is totally different for men.
When the spark goes across between feminine and masculine,
for a man it registers in the unconscious. He doesn't know. He
will come down to earth with a bang and disappear with a
crash into the swamp. He is simply there. He feels he has
touched the earth, but for him this is not so much a knowing
as an unknowing. If a man is looking into the unconscious, he
can only find disorder because for him the balance is in chaos.
But for women the balance is in the order of the conscious.
This is her point of register and as she shifts the balance up,
men can begin to realise their unconscious link with that. It is
because of this evolution of women in consciousness that we

can understand it in this way. But as the balance registers somewhere in his unconscious, his conscious will consequently become stronger. By registering the balance in the unconscious, men will be able to create, to produce something of value in the conscious world.

We are pressurised by modern education towards focused consciousness, and we need this to do the jobs that society persuades us to pursue. But the true creative artists were men who managed to keep contact with diffuse awareness and retain an open channel to the source, the earth. Small wonder then that artists have traditionally gone through conflict and had to experience the pain of outsiders forced outside society in order to create. They have been living out the whole of their being alongside a majority of one-sided people. Since most of the great creators have been men, they were unaware of what caused their creativity to come through. They were able to balance their male and female, but it did not register.

A woman's creativity has until now been in her diffuse awareness. Without focus she was unable to create in the outside world. But now, as her sense of knowing becomes stronger, her ability to create outwardly will also become stronger. She will not create in quite the same way as men, because she is using her animus to focus and therefore focusing in an indirect way, but she can now create outwardly for herself, on her own. As men and women balance out, they will each have the choice in how they wish to create, and as the balance comes finer and finer we should be able to produce greater and greater creativity. We shall have greater access to the source, the Divine Imagination of William Blake. If the female is allowed to reassert herself, the unconscious can begin all over again.

A woman can become creative in her own right, and not simply be the traditional inspiration for a man. But she must also be allowed to keep her fundamental role of helping her man find himself, to keep sight of her natural link with the source in the unconscious. The feminine principle is not to become dominant, but to give the ruling principle the necessary subtlety. And with her new femininity, she can know instinctively what is right. As Irene Claremont de Castillejo said from bibilical reference, the woman must keep the oil in her lamp ready for the bridegroom. The oil is the feminine spirituality in her own psyche and also the symbol of spiritual transformation. The female must be ready for relationship in whatever form that comes, with another person or with work or art or God or the masculine inside her. If she doesn't have oil for the man she loves, she fails him in her role as a woman. Unless she is prepared to accept that feminine spirit in her, to balance the opposites which is necessary for wholeness, she is allowing the masculine in her to take over. But if the oil is ready when the masculine spark comes, "it can burn a flame which is alive and lights our human world. The flame is love and it lights and illuminates our lives only when opposites meet. It can happen in true relationship because in love you have to sacrifice your ego, and this leads to the Self. Or it can happen when a person is balancing out to wholeness because self-realisation also means sacrifice of ego. It can happen equally in men or women where the masculine and feminine meet, but the process of wholeness in men becomes far easier if women play their part. Behind every successful man is a good woman, it is said, and this can still be true. But now she will be there consciously and creatively.

Women's creativity can never be abstract, it is a very personal thing, based on her own subjective experience, not on the objective happenings in the outside world. Her work must always have relevance and meaning to her. To create in the outside world, in man's world, she must have the animus (her masculine quality) in consciousness, but at the same time she must also be true to her own innate nature.

Men will always be responsible for outward creativity, but women have other ways. Men produce forms, but for women it is more subtle, it is a state of being. The male way, since the creativity comes out of chaos, is to create in a more concrete way. For the female, creativity is more abstract, but this does not mean that a woman is less creative. We tend to think this because we put a masculine value on it. Creativity is in being as well as in things produced. Because things are not produced materially this does not mean they do not exist. It is a shift in understanding which our society has not yet recognised. We are persuaded to look for end results, but for a woman her creativity is in the means and not the result. A woman's creativity might be in being happy or watching her children or having tea with friends. Relating is creative. It may be in helping other people to create themselves or in helping the man she loves to create his soul. But because people cannot see the soul, it is said that women cannot create. Creating the right food to create bodies is creative. Creating an atmosphere within which others will find their happiness, is creative. In these terms a woman's creativity is enormous, but we cannot see an atmosphere. Because we cannot quantify the happiness that a woman manages to create in a home, it tends to go unrecognised. Women create beauty and inspiration, but we cannot pick these up.

By being whole, a woman can now choose to create forms as well as atmosphere. Knowing woman has the choice. Whether she is a working psychologist or a mother of six, she doesn't have to prove anything. Her creativity has the best of both worlds. She may be independent in her own right and also enjoy a relationship. It is the animus that drives a woman to prove she is something special and says that the alternative is to become a cabbage. 'Knowing' helps her know that she is trying to prove something to someone who doesn't need proving to. It doesn't matter at all. Whether she prefers to knit in the country in a small cottage or live in the city working at a competitive job, she has already proved her point. She is free. In consciousness the Earth Mother cannot pull her back towards inertia. She need not become a cabbage, she can eat it!

Living is the work a woman has to do. She has to find herself and learn to be. Whatever she does is right because it has to be the sum total of her whole being. It can be done in relationship with her man, because without trying the female gives meaning to what the man is doing. With the knowing that comes from the animus, a woman can relax into being creative without being driven by it. She can still remain in the kitchen and cook because somehow the meaning of this aspiration is communicated to men. Simply by being, she acts as a reminder to him that it is all right if he plays. Life is happy. As she evolves, going more deeply into herself and her contact with the source, she will be more in touch with her senses and she will be happy to create in the habitual female way. By being herself she can create the atmosphere in which a child can be woven and spun in the harmony it needs. The birth of a child takes on a deeper meaning because it allows a deep, conscious relationship between two human beings and not simply the propagation of the species. And if she chooses to work in the outside world instead, where the head and heart values are both available, her maternal urge can be fulfilled in this way too. The love energy which would go into her children may equally be deployed in the products of her work and in watching these grow. She need not feel dissatisfied because she does not have a child. To have a child is to let a soul incarnate on earth, and if a child chooses you to be his parents it will bring that about. If he does not, perhaps you are saying 'please don't choose me'.

The first reaction to 'knowing' is to grab hold of it, afraid to close your eyes in case it goes away. But if you prop up your eyelids with matchsticks the knowing becomes boring and serious, it is simply mouthing an abstract. Knowing says you must trust in being. And once you see it, you must be it. It cannot go away. You must turn your back and walk away, return to being in the world. The overwhelming urge at the first sense of this link with Self is to love and to service, but service to life is not what people think it is. Service is being true to ourselves and living life as truly as we can. By improving the quality of our own life, then we, as a drop in the ocean, are automatically improving the ocean. Service is in being what we are, not in being spiritual or powerful or perfect. Duty is to do the things we enjoy, and if people are helped in the process, that's fine. It is our responsibility to find the balance in being happy in what we do and finding fulfilment, and because we cannot work at anything that doesn't have personal meaning, we will naturally be fulfilled. It is in finding our own balance between going out to do and staying back to be, that we will have an affect on others. Once we are aware of a place out of which we work as human beings, it doesn't matter so much in what way we fulfil the initial vision. The outlets are less important than the making it part of our living and feeling experience. When the vehicle is in reasonable order we can automatically begin to carry on the vision. It may take the rest of our lives, but we can learn to wait.

Once the need to do something *Meaningful* and *Spiritual* is forgotten, we may think we have lost our power, but this is not so. It is simply that we do not feel the power in it. To do something meaningful is the magic of the animus. To let go of that need is to become open and female and human and to allow people to relate to what we are. By being what you are and doing exactly what feels good for you and not for any great meaningful purpose for the cosmos, you are free. You can be creative because you are no longer trying to make yourself creative for ulterior motives. When you no longer care what comes out, the right things come automatically. Whatever happens in the long run will be far more creative.

The danger in the 'consciousness' movement is that people are withdrawing from everyday activities, separating out into their own small community corners. This may have been necessary, but if the idea is to really communicate, this is not the way it should be. To be really conscious of the wholeness of things we need to set it within that wholeness, we need the grain of yeast in the middle of the flour to enable it to ferment. There are many highly-evolved people doing good for humanity in a totally unconscious awareness of what they are doing. They do not need to study or join a group or take a spiritual path; they serve humanity instinctively in a quietly positive way. We are confused into thinking that the everyday, competitive way is wrong, but this is a normal state of expression of the human being. People will go on performing their functions in the old ways. To 'know' is not to convert, but simply to be there, alertly passive.

'Knowing woman' is part of a group fulfilling a particular function which isn't any better or worse than any other. Just different. She is performing a certain kind of role in the economy. People are all at different levels of growth and on different levels of awareness corresponding to their temperament. According to the Jungian psychologist Toni Wolff there are four different female archetypes; all women have the potential for all of them, but respond to different ones. Their temperament is more aligned with one than the others. The *Earth Mother*, which was represented in the Taurean age, is the woman who doesn't depend on being conscious of her own motivations. She is the dark and light aspect in everything associated with the mother. She is feeling-oriented and undifferentiated; collective wisdom rather than individual wisdom. The *Hetaira* woman is the opposite from the maternal mother. She represents the arts and culture, the aesthetic and intellect. She is instability, the butterfly-bubble. She relates to men for their own sake, not as the father of her child. She is the companion whose relationships with men are all-important. She is the reflection of his anima, his flatterer. The *Amazon* woman, the woman in the last Piscean Age is also an earth figure but in a different way. As the Virgo earth figure, the opposite pole to the Pisces male, she is able to function on the material level and make it possible for men to do so too. She is the capable earth figure, but in close relation with the mother and a creative inspiration. In business she is an individual, the sort of woman we are experiencing now. The *Medium* woman interprets. She is the figure who senses the whiff of currents and can communicate them. She is the High Priestess who has to know because she has to translate. She can be more conscious.

Each age is equated with a state of conciousness. The role of the masculine is to give form to the dominant values of the age, to give it realisation. The feminine role in each age is to ground it and make it of value, to restore the dignity of the individual. The female wants to act as a catalyst and bring together, and her opposite values must be integrated into the dominating role. For the last 2000 years during the Arian and Piscean ages, the feminine has been degraded. There was an overvaluing of the spirit and an undervaluing of the earth, and women were relegated to the basement. But the Aquarian Age will turn this on its head, because it is a time of earth, a time of man's becoming. 'Man know thyself'. The Age of Aquarius will be a further age of science and logic but the role of Leo, diametrically opposed, will be to bring in her playfulness and humour as an antidote. She will provide both a spontaneous counterpoint to the mass of information that is now coming in, and add a sense of meaning to it all. She is not so much happiness as joy, like the sun card in the tarot pack. This will be the age for 'knowing woman', for the Medium, but she cannot do this until the restoration of the dignity of the female symbol, otherwise she will be lost to the scientific age. For men to take things like astrology and the psyche and organise and quantify them is to drive the soul out of them. All these mysteries will be reduced to concepts unless the balance of 'knowing' says there is something that cannot be measured or articulated living through them. If the polarity of Leo is undervalued there is danger that the world will continue the way it is going. There will be no room for individual creativity.

Women have always given men a feeling of continuity, the sense that no matter what happens on the hunt, her house is clean and tidy and there is always a meal waiting. Now she will give him the feeling that life is fun, and through her own creativity in writing, painting or dancing, she can be his inspiration. Leos never grow up, they are perpetually irrepressible. The earth is the art of the ridiculous and there is humour underlying everything. Women can perpetuate the cosmic joke. A woman says one thing and means another, she is contradictory and so is the earth. She can give the joke meaning because you can only see a joke if you see the interconnections. If not, you miss the punchline.

There is love of God in every age and the need to unite with the source has led to many varieties of religion, depending on the psychological conditions of the people concerned. We must consider what we need now. The passing age of Pisces was a masculine age, and it was natural that religion should go outward into the spiritual in male dominated religions. An attribute of Pisces, too, is the ethos of suffering; that suffering is good for the soul and that life is a vale of tears. But Pisces is a dual sign, symbolised by two fish swimming in opposite directions. To swim forward symbolises the male attribute of logic and progress and going forward. It is female to look back and it is the woman in myth who looks back with nostalgia to the Golden Age. In the Piscean Age, dominated by the masculine, there was also an unconscious pull in the opposite direction to the conscious. The Piscean Age brought an apparently male religion, but aware people have always known there was something else. The manifestation on the surface was sufficient for many people, but there was always this other thing that no one could quite put their finger on and which tended to come out as mysterious. The duality of Pisces represents an underlying occult sense, but because the unconscious female is cloying; it is the thing Pisces wants least. It is this perhaps that has led to the occult breaking through as an inner culture, a searching for something that has so far been denied.

The female of the age came in in the wrong way because men were afraid of her cloying unconscious nature. In the Christian religion, and even more obviously in the Catholic religion, the female was represented by the acceptable Virgin Mary. But the proper power the female lies beyond Mary, and perhaps the rightful female has been moving along quietly all the time. If she could be brought into consciousness, she need not be occult and cloying. Perhaps we must allow the Piscean female to come through in consciousness before the success of the New Age can be guaranteed. Rudolf Steiner said that the coming of Christ marked the mid-point in evolution of the human soul, its lowest descent from the spiritual to the material, from which, by the Christ Impulse, we begin to ascend to spiritual knowledge. Perhaps with the acknowledgement of the female in us all, we can begin that ascent in earnest.

The need to search for something more is a powerful feeling in so many people. Which is why the legends and myths surrounding King Arthur and his Knights and the Glastonbury romances have so strongly caught the world imagination. People are pulled to Glastonbury because they feel certain it has magic energy and that there is something there which provides a mssing link. The search for the Holy Grail has become a cult. Legend assumes the Grail to be a holy relic, the actual cup used by Christ at the Last Supper and brought by Joseph of Arimathea to England. But the

Grail was not always holy as it is under its Christian tag; this was an afterthought. As Geoffrey Ashe explains in *King Arthur's Avalon*, the Grail appeared in myths of British and other cultures a long time before this. It began as a talisman. The grail was a vessel or bowl and was conceived as a source of food, as a cauldron of plenty and inspiration. In ancient mythological terms the Grail was a mysterious and miraculous source of physical well-being.

In King Arthur's day the Grail passed to the British church, and since then it has enveloped a Christian mystery with the possibility of an insight which no one has thought of: an opening of a special door. Arthur was a mixture of fact and fiction; his birth was supposedly due to Merlin's magic. In Glastonbury, which is said to be Arthur's Avalon, the legends centre on the ruined Abbey, which was supposed to have been the oldest Christian foundation in Britain, and particularly around the Lady Chapel which was built on the site of the original wattle Church. This was the starting point of British Christianity, but the official Church mistrusted the Grail because when Arthurian romances began to catch on, the 'other' Christianity, the Celtic 'something else' stayed with it.

According to Geoffrey Ashe, the Grail has many properties. It is the source of a secret life and even when spoken about in a highly spiritual way, it still has the attributes of its primitive spiritual function, as cornucopia. It holds the magic to produce all nourishment needed. It is food for the soul, a bowl of inspiration and symbolically the object of all man's aspirations. It contains 'the daily bread by which God sustains man on his earthly pilgrimage towards heaven and the incarnation and atonement by which God draws man to himself. The sacrament by which God sanctifies and enlightens him.' A cup or vessel is a symbol of the feminine, of earth and nature, and all the needs of the Grail were seemingly fulfilled by the Virgin Mary. Britain was the first country to honour her and thus the Grail became associated with the Mary cult. The medieval Christians referred to the Virgin Mary as the Cauldron, or source of inspiration. Geoffrey Ashe goes on to explain that in 1190 the mystic Robert de Borron suggested that the life-giving vessel was a Christian object, but also that it was keeping something back, and that when the revelation occurred it would be significant to the Blessed Trinity. First there is The Father, then the Son Made Flesh. Is it possible, I wonder, that the third, the Holy Ghost, is to be not an individual, but something arising from within humanity as a whole? A Daughter Made Flesh.

By Arthur's time the grail was lost, but it is apparently still in Britain. To achieve the Grail, as Galahad did, one has to undergo an experience which no one else can describe. The Christian Grail is lost and may be found again. At one time, the Holy Mystery was openly evident in Britain and if it could be found again it would mean the recovery of a long-lost glory. Hints that the Virgin Mary replaced the pagan Mother Goddess are behind the magic cup, and the Grail cult is influenced by its devotion to her. But the cult of the Mother Goddess was very strong in Britain when the Grail first appeared and it is possible perhaps that Mary is not the female the Grail symbolises. Perhaps the female, the Daughter Made Flesh, has yet to appear in consciousness. It is the male way to look outward in his search for the Grail, to search for an object. Could that 'object' be a state of being? There is still a sense that Arthur's shrine will witness some kind of rebirth, that there is something to be awakened, a dormant power. Something personal to Albion, which will as William Blake suggested, become great again.

And the I that is me ...

I felt I had something to do. A role to play. I did not know how or when, but as each stage of the last three years took me into more and more strange and unknown realms, I knew that at the end I had to produce a tangible form of that 'knowing'. I thought, too, that once I had found my expression of this experience, I would have found my life's work.

Gradually it became increasingly obvious that my path had always been as a communicator, and through synchronistic meetings and past hopes, I began to know that the product must be a book. My 'Saturn hit' at twenty had given me an experience which as a young magazine writer I felt I could translate in order to help younger people through similar experience. Somehow, in the back of my mind, I had always known that when I had exhausted this experience I might be able to cross another threshold and find a way to pass on that knowledge. But a book! How on earth could I describe in verbal terms a non-verbal concept? Consciousness is invisible.

But the certainty grew and the sychronistic bits and pieces kept on coming together. People, books and ideas leapt at me. Nothing that came was wasted, it all had relevance. It was desolate, and exciting, but suddenly the germ of an idea was there. I caught at it in desperation, and almost unbelievably, it grew. Over the previous two years I had given up work, home and income to follow my certainty, and then, although I doubted it every second day, I realised that everything I chose to do brought another piece of the jigsaw into view.

I knew I could do nothing else until it was done, but some days it seemed an impossible endeavour. On others, it was so right I wondered how I could doubt. I did my research and thinking virtually alone. I value friends above all else, but for two years I was unable to share my thoughts – it was almost as though people could destroy that precious germ if I gave it away.

Finally, one day I knew it was right to begin, where before

I could positively not have moved. Suddenly the pieces of the puzzle began to fit into place. After all the doubt and uncertainty the baby, my book, *had* to be born. There was no alternative – as there had been no alternative since that first 'pull' of the 'personal call'. I locked myself away for four months to write. Nothing else was important or relevant until it was finished.

And now, I am empty. It has been like an exorcism and the burden of those years has fallen away. It is as though they never existed. The certainty of my knowing seems also to have gone, the book seems hardly mine. It is as though I am free again to be myself, to begin my life, in freedom. I have not found my life's work, but neither have I boundaries. The old has gone, and there is only the new. At this stage it does not matter which way I go, but I know that practical things, which I continue to worry about, will be all right whichever way I go. I do not need to be involved in 'consciousness' or 'alternatives'. Only with life, in whichever way it goes for me. Because now, I am ... just me.

Of course we all need further understanding. It was the need to find an answer that began the search and it is this that keeps us on the path towards an answer. We must constantly assess and observe and use our problems, to provide greater insights into the underlying source. At the beginning there is a deep need for a sense of purpose, but this need leads to the point where the only purpose is to be. To know this is to bring in an even greater sense of that purpose, because man will always want to explore and evolve that need to be. Everything is like a skin over something else. Knowledge and experience are connected and there is infinite life in them both. There is an appropriateness in all connections.

Knowing does not make life simpler, just much much bigger.

Holford, Somerset 1977.

Books that helped to clear the Path

LIZ GREENE

Bailey, Alice. *A Treatise on the Seven Rays: Esoteric Astrology.* Lucis Press, 1968.

Bailey, Alice. *A Treatise on the Seven Rays: Esoteric Psychology.* Two Volumes. Lucis Press, 1967 & 1970.

Grant, Joan. *Winged Pharoah.* Sphere, 1973.

Harding, Esther M. *The Way of All Women.* Jung Foundation, 1970.

Jung, Carl G. *Memories, Dreams, Reflections.* Fontana, 1967.

Jung, Carl G. *Psychology and Alchemy.* Routledge, 1976.

Renault, Mary. *The King Must Die.* New English Library, 1976.

Wickes, Frances Gillespy. *The Inner World of Childhood.* Coventure Books, 1977.

Yeats, W.B. *Collected Poems.* Macmillan, 1950.

LORRAINE GILL

Badt, Kurt. *The Art of Cézanne.* Faber and Faber, 1965.

Berger, John. *The Success and Failure of Picasso.* Penguin, 1963.

Castaneda, Carlos. *The Teachings of Don Juan.* Penguin, 1970.

Chardin, Pierre Teilhard de. *Hymn of the Universe.* Fontana, 1969.

Jung, Carl G. *Memories, Dreams, Reflections.* Fontana, 1967.

Nietzsche, Friedrich. *Thus Spake Zarathustra.* Penguin, 1969.

Pearce, Joseph Chilton. *The Crack in the Cosmic Egg.* Lyrebird Press, 1973.

Reti, Ladislao (ed.) *Unknown Leonardo.* McGraw Hill, 1974.

LYNICE YATES

Castaneda, Carlos. *A Separate Reality.* Penguin, 1973.
Castaneda, Carlos. *Journey to Ixtlan.* Penguin, 1975.
Castaneda, Carlos. *Tales of Power.* Hodder and Stoughton, 1975.
Gibran, Kahlil. *Jesus, Son of Man.* Heinemann, 1976.
Lytton, Edward Bulwer. *Zanoni.* Multimedia, 1971.
Pirsig, Robert. *Zen and the Art of Motorcycle Maintenance.* Bodley Head, 1974.
Steiner, Rudolf. *Knowledge of the Higher Worlds'* The Steiner Press, 1969.
Steiner, Rudolf. *A Modern Art of Education.* The Steiner Press, 1972.

ISOBEL McGILVRAY

Adam, Michael. *Man is a Little World.* Ark Press, 1968.
Berne, Eric. *What Do You Say After You Say Hello.* Corgi, 1976.
Castillejo, Irene Claremont de. *Knowing Woman.* Hodder and Stoughton, 1973.
Franz, Marie-Louise von. *Feminine in Fairy Tales.* Spring Publications, 1976.
Groddeck, Georg W. *Book of the It.* Vision Press, 1976.
Long, Max Freedom. *The Secret Science Behind Miracles'.* Huna Research Publication, 1954.
Koestler, Arthur. *The Ghost in the Machine.* Hutchinson, 1967.
Liedloff, Jean. *The Continuum Concept.* Futura, 1975.
Rajneesh, Bhagwan S. *Way of the White Cloud.* Harper and Row, 1975.
Simeons, Albert T. *Man's Presumptious Brain.* Longmans, 1960.

DIANA BECCHETTI

Assagioli, Roberto. *Act of Will.* Wildwood, 1974.
Assagioli, Roberto. *Psychosynthesis.* Turnstone Press, 1975.
Bailey, Alice. Collected Works by Lucis Trust Press from 1958.

Challoner, H.K. *The Path of Healing.* Theosophical Publishing House, 1972.

Chardin, Pierre Teilhard de. *Hymn of the Universe.* Fontana, 1969.

Gray, Martin. *A Book of Life.* Talmy Franklin, 1975.

Gray, Martin. *For Those I Loved.* Bodley Head, 1973.

Moustakas, Clark E. *The Self.* Harper and Row, 1975.

Perls, Frederick. *Gestalt Therapy Verbatim.* Bantam, 1972.

Prather, Hugh. *Notes to Myself.* Lyrebird Press, 1973.

Radhakrishnan, S. *The Bhagavadgita.* Harper and Row, 1975.

Ramacharaka, Yogi. *Raja Yoga.* Yoga Publications, 1972.

Rogers, Carl R. *Freedom to Learn.* Merril, 1975.

Spangler, David. *Revelation: the Birth of a New Age.* The Findhorn Foundation, 1974.

Sorokin, Pitirim A. *The Ways and Power of Love.* Beacon, 1954.

Stevens, Barry. *Don't Push the River.* Real People Press, 1970.

Underhill, Evelyn. *Mysticism.* Methuen, 1960.

ANNIE WILSON

Adam, Michael. *Man is a Little World.* Ark Press, 1968.

Ashe, Geoffrey. *King Arthur's Avalon.* Fontana, 1973.

Assagioli, Roberto. *Act of Will.* Wildwood, 1974.

Assagioli, Roberto. *Psychosynthesis.* Turnstone Press. 1975.

Barlow, Wilfred. *The Alexander Principle.* Arrow Books, 1975.

Castaneda, Carlos. *The Teachings of Don Juan.* Penguin, 1973.

Castaneda, Carlos. *Journey to Ixtlan.* Penguin, 1975.

Castillejo, Irene Claremont de. *Knowing Woman.* Hodder and Stoughton, 1973.

Franz, Marie-Louise von. *Feminine in Fairy Tales.* Spring Publications, 1976.

Harding, Esther M. *The Way of All Women.* Jung Foundation, 1970

Liedloff, Jean. *The Continuum Concept.* Futura, 1975.

Rola, Stanislas Klossowski de. *The Secret Art of Alchemy.* Thames and Hudson, 1973.

Stevens, Wallace. *Selected Poems.* Faber and Faber, 1953.

Wilson, Colin. *New Pathways in Psychology.* A Mentor Book, 1972.